Armenia
IN CRISIS
THE 1988
EARTHQUAKE

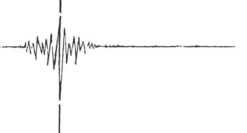

The publication of this book was made possible by grants from
the University of Massachusetts, Lowell, and
the Armenian General Benevolent Union—Alex Manoogian Cultural Fund.

Pierre Verluise

Armenia
IN CRISIS
THE 1988
EARTHQUAKE

Translated by LEVON CHORBAJIAN

With a Foreword by GÉRARD CHALIAND

Wayne State University Press   Detroit

LIBRARY OF CONGRESS CATALOGING IN
PUBLICATION DATA

Verluise, Pierre.
  [Arménie, la fracture. English]
  Armenia in crisis : the 1988 earthquake / Pierre Verluise ;
translated by Levon Chorbajian ; with a foreword by Gérard
Chaliand.
     p.   cm.
  Includes bibliographical references and index.
  ISBN 0–8143–2527–0 (alk. paper). —
  ISBN 0–8143–2528–9 (pbk.: alk. paper)
  1. Armenia (Republic)—Politics and government. 2. Earth-
quakes—Armenia (Republic). 3. Disaster relief—Armenia (Repub-
lic). 4. Armenians—Azerbaijan—Nagorno–Karabakh. 5. Nagorno-
Karabakh (Azerbaijan)—Ethnic relations. 6. Armenia (Republic)—
Ethnic relations. I. Chorbajian, Levon II. Title.
DK687.V4713   1995   94–23422
956.6'2038—dc20

DESIGNER: S. R. TENENBAUM

COVER ART: The interior wall of a collapsed apartment building

SPECIAL ACKNOWLEDGMENT:

Photographs courtesy of Zoryan Institute, Cambridge, Massachusetts.

Contents

PART III

THE POLITICAL DIMENSION 79

Preface to the English Edition

LEVON CHORBAJIAN

1986–1987

In the spring of 1986 I was awarded a Fulbright Senior Lectureship to teach sociology at Yerevan State University in what was still the Armenian S.S.R. It was an exciting award, in part because sociology had been a suspect and outlaw discipline in the Soviet Union for decades. Few Western sociologists had ever had an opportunity to interact with colleagues and students in a Soviet university to see how the discipline was defined and practiced.[1]

I also had a less professional and more personal interest as an American-Armenian. For many Armenians in the West, Soviet Armenia represented a bittersweet legacy. On the one hand, the territory of Soviet Armenia was one of the few Armenian communities to survive World War I with its population largely intact. As the only territory bearing the name Armenia, it also underwent considerable agricultural, industrial, and cultural development during the years of Soviet rule, and for many Armenians outside its borders, Soviet Armenia was a source of pride. But these facts were tempered by other realities including Armenia's loss of its two-year interlude of independence to the Soviets in 1920 and the loss of traditional Armenian lands to Turkey and the neighboring Soviet republic of Azerbaijan in 1920 and

1921. The controversies surrounding these events had divided Armenian communities in the diaspora for decades.[2]

Additional political problems were generated by U.S.–Soviet hostilities predating the Cold War and then by the long years of the Cold War itself. As a result, the Armenian homeland was rendered distant and inaccessible for most Armenians in the United States and, to a lesser degree, Armenians elsewhere in the West. Limited possibilities for tourism opened up for U.S. citizens only in the late 1950s, and the Fulbright program only began assigning exchange professors to Yerevan in 1978.

The literature was also scant. Russocentrism dominated scholarly and journalistic works on the Soviet Union, and one often looked in vain for even a superficial treatment of Soviet minorities. There were a few propaganda volumes extolling Soviet Armenian achievements[3] and a few émigré accounts focusing on life in an authoritarian state.[4] Each genre had serious shortcomings, and questions about the organization and workings of Soviet Armenian social institutions and the broad outlines and nuances of daily life went begging for answers. My wife and I were anxious to begin sharing our lives with our Soviet Armenian counterparts, and to begin filling in some of the gaps.[5]

When we arrived in Yerevan in early September 1986, we got lucky. Nearly all visitors to the Soviet Union were housed in one of two sorts of places, dormitories and hotels. For people like ourselves, interested in how Soviet citizens in a minority republic defined and lived their daily lives, both options offered only limited possibilities. In dormitories, for the most part, you meet foreign students and visiting academics, and conversations tend to revolve around aspects of life in one's country of origin and perceptions of local life and politics as seen through foreign eyes. The social fare at hotels is considerably more varied—tourists, visiting athletic teams and dance troupes and the like, and locals plying black market goods and sex, exchanging local currencies for dollars, and seeking quickie marriages as an escape route to the West. Neither setting interested us greatly other than as a place to stay, though we were prepared to make the best of our housing assignment. This proved unnecessary because we were given a three-room apartment in an ordinary apartment building in a typical neighborhood in Yerevan. I suspect that our housing assignment had something to do with the fact that there were six of us—my wife and I and our four children, then aged 6, 5, 3, and 9 months. In any case, we had our housing assignment, we would be living with the people.

Among our neighbors were construction workers and foremen, teachers, housewives, retirees, engineers, childcare workers, secretaries, students, a plant manager, a musician, a family and wedding photographer, a bus mechanic, and a boxing coach, among others. It was not high society, which would not have suited us, but it was a nice cross section of middle-level professionals and blue-collar workers. Because my wife and I and the older children had some knowledge of the Armenian language, and because the children were young in this child-centered culture, we were warmly received by our neighbors. By the end of the first week, largely because of friendly neighborly advice on getting through the various school and medical bureaucracies, the oldest child was enrolled in the first grade at the local school and the two middle children were attending the daycare center in our apartment complex.

We would, of course, always be visitors from another place because the lives of our neighbors differed in significant ways from our own. Unlike them, we had no memories of the Soviet World War II experience or of Stalinism. We were also there for a limited amount of time, ten months, and after that we would be leaving. On the other hand, we were, of necessity, sharing important aspects of our lives with our neighbors as we shopped, cooked, cleaned, and got around the city as they did. Slowly our language skills improved as did our skills for daily living. We were beginning to feel a part of the local scene.

One day, a month into our stay, when it was still summery and hot, an incident marked this transition for me. I was returning from the open market carrying heavy bags of fruits, vegetables, and rice. It was about a two kilometer walk from our apartment, and even though, downhill, I was sweaty and tired. At one point, I stopped next to an air-conditioned bus full of tourists. The driver had stopped for a red light. I looked up and back and saw a line of faces, blond, blue-eyed, and fair—and, above all, comfortable. As I stood there with the narrow handles on the shopping bags cutting into my palms, I understood why my neighbors spoke of tourists with a mixture of disdain and envy and why they had been quick to distinguish my wife and me as people who had "come to work."

Some of the tourists, I noticed, were gazing idly about and others were chatting with their neighbors. Still others were looking intently at me, scrutinizing my bags and demeanor for clues, perhaps, to life in this, their chosen vacation spot. In that instant, I had become an object, which I didn't care for, and I had also become, for those who had no way of knowing any better, a local.

Granted, we can make too much of a busload of East German or Polish tourists mistaking my large brown eyes and dark complexion for those of a native. That would certainly be the case if it were not for our developing social network at the university and in our housing complex. Most of our evenings were spent visiting and hosting our neighbors, participating in rituals of tea and coffee drinking (surprisingly elegant, even in the plain and often cramped physical setting of people's apartments), vodka and cognac toasting, and the sharing of food.[6] Both the small, repetitive events of daily life and the larger benchmarks such as weddings, births, baptisms, illnesses, and deaths served as venues for the expression and growth of solidarity and friendship. For this reason the tourists had erred only partially, because while we were outsiders observing, we were also insiders participating in a complex society that was experiencing the beginning ripples of rapid and unforeseen social changes.

We made many lasting friendships during the year, and despite some material discomforts, our stay in Yerevan was a rewarding and memorable one.

1988

The year 1988 was a memorable year of a different sort. In the summer of 1987, First Secretary of the Soviet Communist Party, Mikhail Gorbachev publicly criticized the Communist leadership of Armenia for the slow pace of reform in the republic. Before long, the irony of this rebuke would become clear to one and all.

In late February 1988, Yerevan was the scene of unprecedented mass demonstrations of reportedly up to one million
people on a single day. The protesters had rallied peacefully in
support of Armenians in Mountainous (Nagorno) Karabagh, a
historically Armenian enclave that had been ceded by the Soviets
to neighboring Azerbaijan in 1921, despite the fact that the
population of the territory was over 90 percent Armenian in the
early 1920s.[7] The Karabagh issue was at the center of the protests, but there were other issues that had brought people into
the streets. These included corruption in the Armenian Communist Party, the slow pace of democratization, and serious
environmental problems in the republic.

Over the course of the next nine months, the region was in
turmoil. In response to the protests, Armenians in the Azerbaijani industrial city of Sumgait were subjected to a vicious pogrom.[8] Yerevan and Stepanagert (the capital of Mountainous
Karabagh) were the sites of demonstrations, marches, general
strikes, boycotts, hunger strikes, and vigils. The Soviet government imposed military occupation and martial law in Armenia.
In the late spring, the First Secretaries of the Armenian and
Azerbaijani Communist Parties were dismissed by Gorbachev
and replaced. In July, Armenian protesters seized the international airport in Yerevan for a brief period until it was retaken by
crack Soviet troops. In the fall, Armenians living in Azerbaijan
were expelled, and the Armenians retaliated against Azerbaijanis
in Armenia in the first of a series of forced expulsions that
would clear each republic of its targeted minority population.

The year ended with the devastating earthquake which left
tens of thousands dead and much of northwest Armenia, including the republic's second largest city, Leninakan, in ruins.[9]

MAY 1989

Because of the timing of our departure from Yerevan in
late June 1987, we were forced to follow the dramatic events of
1988 from afar. It was an agonizing separation for us, since we
had visited Leninakan, and we had many friends whose extended families lived there. What had been their fate?

I was finally able to return to Yerevan for a two-week visit in May of 1989, this time alone. It was six months after the earthquake. I wanted to reestablish old ties and find answers to the many questions posed by the historic events of 1988. One of the people I sought out was Vahinag, a 38-year-old construction foreman who lived in our old apartment building. When I located him, he told me he was going to Leninakan the next morning for the day and offered to take me along.

We set off early the next morning with his crew chief Mihran. On the outskirts of Yerevan, Vahinag stopped the car near a dry, rocky riverbed to view the remains of a Yugoslav Antonov-12 cargo plane that had crashed bringing relief supplies into Armenia. The crew of seven had perished. An old woman in a sort of makeshift shrine was there selling roses. She hinted that pieces of souvenir wreckage could be had for a price.

As we continued on toward Leninakan, Vahinag explained that he had driven there immediately after hearing of the earthquake and was one of the first people to arrive from Yerevan. When he saw the scale of the destruction, he rushed back to the capital to round up his crew. They returned to Leninakan with Vahinag's construction crane, which they would need to carry out rescue efforts. The trip back took hours on the now jammed roadway. He and his crew worked for twenty-four hours searching the remains of a collapsed factory building for survivors. As in many of the rescue efforts described by Verluise, Vahinag and his crew discovered only bodies among the rubble. They later worked with a team of American rescue workers on another collapsed structure with the same results. According to Vahinag:

> It was very discouraging. We went there to help and only found bodies. I never thought I could stand work like that, but it had to be done and we did it.

On the outskirts of Leninakan, as we approached from the south, we saw few signs of damage, but as we continued to drive, scenes of destruction came into view and then quickly dominated the landscape. Badly damaged and collapsed buildings were everywhere. Even though I had read about the earthquake and had seen pictures, the reality was nightmarish and shocking.

Our first stop was a cemetery where we visited the graves of two of Vahinag's first cousins. They were buried among many fresh graves, some unmarked, most with makeshift markers or new headstones. The victims were old and young, male and female. They all shared the common inscription: 7 December 1988.

Many of the survivors were housed in yurt-shaped tents, and we passed their olive-drab encampments that dotted the city. Others survivors, more fortunate, had been given trailers, and some, because they did not want to give them up or because they had no place to go, still occupied their apartments in badly damaged buildings that were slated for demolition.

Vahinag's kin were living in a two-room trailer in what used to be the courtyard of their apartment complex. The row of apartment buildings, now on the demolition list, stood twenty feet away. On the other side of the courtyard trailer park were the shells of buildings and piles of rubble waiting to be cleared away.

Our hosts, Albert and Zvart, greeted us warmly and welcomed us into their new home, apologizing for its small size and sparse furnishings. Albert and Zvart were in their fifties, and they lost their two adult sons in the disaster. It was their graves we had visited at the cemetery. On Zvart's side of the family, eighteen people had perished. Joining us on this day were an unmarried daughter, the widowed daughter-in-law, and two grandchildren aged six and nine.

In a slow and deliberate manner, Albert spoke at length about his experiences during the earthquake and his views on many related issues. He began by talking about the family gathering on the day of the earthquake, which was to be a send-off for the younger son who was leaving for his two-year stint in the army. When the earthquake hit, the two brothers and a friend fled the apartment and were killed when the stairs and foyer collapsed. Albert told me matter-of-factly that had they left only seconds earlier, they would have made it safely to the street.

Albert and his wife were saved because they were in their car, still on the way when the first tremor hit. Ophelia, the daughter-in-law, had gone for a walk with the children. She told me she clutched her children with one arm and a tree with the other. The tree was rocked back and forth, and the three of them with it. She said she saw the apartment building lifted off of its foundation by the force of the tremor. I wondered how many thousands of stories of coincidences and seconds and split seconds had been told throughout the city in the months since the catastrophe.

Later, Albert drove Vahinag, Mihran, and myself around the city. He showed us the collapsed hospital complex where doctors, nurses, and patients alike had died within seconds. He railed against corrupt Communist Party officials who had been selling some of the relief supplies donated from abroad. He also pointed out buildings that sustained little or no damage. They were typically one or two stories high and dated from the 1920s and 1930s or earlier, from tsarist times. Albert launched an impassioned attack, as I would hear others do, on the Party and Communist leaders from Khrushchev to Gorbachev who have "moved the country backwards." "How is it," he asked rhetorically, "that seventy years ago people knew how to build to withstand powerful tremors, but cannot do so now?"

Finally, Albert spoke of Mountainous Karabagh. For him, the poorly designed and constructed apartment buildings and Mountainous Karabagh served a dual symbols of the system's lack of commitment to justice and its insensitivity to human needs. At one point Albert waved his hand in front of him in a wide sweep, pointing to the destruction everywhere around us and said:

> Look at what we have after seventy years of Communism. Nothing! What do we have to lose? Maybe it is time for us to go our own way, to start over.

It was a sentiment I had heard from only two or three people in 1987. On this trip, I was hearing it from many people from all walks of life. Mountainous Karabagh and the earthquake had clearly changed things deeply and irreversibly.[10]

TRANSLITERATION NOTE AND ACKNOWLEDGMENTS

For the purposes of transliteration I have relied mainly on Randall K. Barry's American Library Association and Library of Congress system for the transliteration of non-Roman scripts. The main exception to Barry's schema occurs in the case of particular orthographies that have become commonplace in the West, including the print media. Thus Yerevan is preferred over Erivan, Nakhichevan over Nakhijevan, Etchmiadzin over Ejmiatsin, etc.

In the process of preparing this translation I became indebted to a number of concerned and helpful individuals. Sr. Alphonsa Bedrosian, Director of the Armenian Sisters' Academy of Lexington, Massachusetts, Mr. Krikor Keussayan, editor with the Baikar Association of Watertown, Massachusetts, and Dr. Geoffrey Goshgarian of the University of Burgundy assisted willingly and capably when called upon. Laura Yardumian of the Zoryan Institute in Cambridge, Massachusetts, helped me in collecting the photographs. I would also like to thank Dr. Joseph Garreau of the University of Massachusetts, Lowell and Mr. Markar Melkonian of Chicago, Illinois, for their support. Mr. Edmund Azadian, Director of the Alex Manoogian Cultural Fund of Taylor, Michigan, and Dr. William T. Hogan, Chancellor of the University of Massachusetts, Lowell deserve special mention for their appreciation of the value of Pierre Verluise's work and of the publication of its English translation. The small grants made by each of them were essential to the publication of this work.

My wife and children deserve special mention for their unwavering support for this project and the sacrifices they were willing to make to assure its completion.

NOTES

1. For a discussion of Soviet sociology see Vladimir Shlapentokh, *The Politics of Sociology in the Soviet Union* (Boulder, CO, 1987).

2. For thorough discussion of this issue in east-coast Armenian-American communities, see Jenny Phillips, *Symbol, Myth, and Rhetoric: The Politics of Culture in an Armenian-American Population* (New York, 1989) and Anny Bakalian, *Armenian-Americans: From Being to Feeling Armenian* (New Brunswick, NJ, 1993), chapter 2, "The Church and Politics," pp. 89–178.

3. Charles Aznakian Vertanes, *Armenia Reborn* (New York, 1947).

4. Hagop Jack Touryantz, *Search for a Homeland* (New York, 1987).

5. Part of our experience may be found in Levon Chorbajian, "Quelques constatations sur l'Arménie soviétique," *Les Temps Modernes*, vol. 43 (July-August, 1988), pp. 152–163 and Levon Chorbajian, "For the Masses: Television in the Armenian S.S.R.," *The Armenian Review*, vol. 42 (1989), pp. 37–52. An older, but still useful, study dealing with social issues in Soviet Armenia is Mary Kilbourne Matossian, *The Impact of Soviet Policies in Armenia* (Westport, CT, 1981, originally 1962). A concise history has been provided by Ronald Grigor Suny, *Armenia in the 20th Century* (Chico, CA, 1983).

6. Though ritual toasting in Armenia differs from toasting in neighboring Georgia, there are strong similarities. For an analysis of the latter, see Dee Ann Holisky, "The Rules of the *Supra* or How To Drink in Georgian," *The Annual of the Society for the Study of Caucasia* 1 (1989), pp. 22–40.

7. A history of Mountainous Karabagh may be found in Levon Chorbajian, Patrick Donabedian, and Claude Mutafian, *The Caucasian Knot: The History and Geopolitics of Nagorno–Karabagh* (London, 1994). A revealing Azerbaijani account is found in George Bournoutian, *A History of Qarabagh: An Annotated Translation of Mirza Jamal Javanshir Qarabaghi's Turikh-e Qarabagh* (Costa Mesa, CA, 1994).

8. See Samvel Shahmuratian, ed., *The Sumgait Tragedy: Eyewitness Accounts* (New Rochelle, NY, 1990).

9. In Soviet times, the city was named after Lenin. In tsarist times, it was called Alexandropol after Tsar Alexander I. The Armenian name, to which it has reverted, is Gumri. For the sake of consistency, Leninakan is used throughout.

10. The Soviet response to the earthquake called for new thinking in other contexts as well. Noam Chomsky, a distinguished critic of U.S. foreign policy, notes the Pentagon's frantic efforts to justify escalated military expenditures in light of Soviet arms reduction initiatives and information revealed by the Armenian earthquake:

> strategic analyst, William V. Kennedy of the U.S. Army War College warns of a terrible discovery revealing that intelligence assessments for the past thirty-five years were far from the mark and severely underestimated the Soviet threat. U.S. intelligence had believed all along that the Soviet Union had "the most elaborate, best organized and equipped civil defense system on earth—so elaborate that it might provide the Soviet Union with a major, perhaps decisive, advantage in a nuclear conflict." But the Armenian earthquake showed that the assessment was wrong. It revealed "inefficiency on so vast a scale that any U.S. state governor or federal official who presided over such chaos would have been lucky to escape lynching by now"—a great surprise to U.S. intelligence, apparently, though hardly to anyone with a minimal familiarity with the Soviet Union. This discovery, Kennedy continues, "is staggering in its implications." . . . The danger is "that a Soviet leadership that saw carefully laid plans going awry and the fires of nationalism spreading throughout the realm could panic into a desperate international venture"—the "wounded bear" theory, some call it. The Armenian earthquake confirmed our worst fears: the Soviet Union has no civil defense capacity at all, hence no capacity for a first strike with relative impunity as the hawks had been ominously warning for years.

Noam Chomsky, *Necessary Illusions: Thought Control in Democratic Societies* (Boston, 1989), pp. 184–185.

Introduction

LEVON CHORBAJIAN

THE SETTING

Armenia occupies a mountainous and high-plain portion of the land bridge linking the Black and Caspian Seas on the frontier of Europe and Asia. This region was conquered by the expanding Russian Empire in the late eighteenth and early nineteenth centuries. In 1918 the region's three largest nationalities, the Armenians, the Azerbaijanis, and the Georgians, took advantage of the turmoil of the early years of the Bolshevik Revolution and declared independence.[1] Within three years, these three fledgling states were Sovietized and for the next seventy years remained as minority republics within the Soviet Union. With the collapse of the Soviet state in late 1991, all three once again asserted their independence.

This area, known as the Transcaucasus, and the contiguous area to the north, the North Caucasus, are home to one of the world's most complex ethnic and linguistic mosaics. Cultural and linguistic differences are layered among indigenous Christian and Moslem communities. In addition, class conflicts have arisen and taken on an ethnic/religious dimension due to differing rates of ethnic group development and patterns of integration into industrializing social structures over the past 150 years.[2] When we consider that the Russians, Ottoman Turks, British, and others have sought to influence and control the region by catering to certain groups and playing them off against others, it should not be surprising that relationships among peoples in the region have often been contentious and sometimes violent.[3] This was true during the 1905 Russian Revolution. It was true during the first years of the Bolshevik Revolution. And it is true today.

Beneath the Soviet rhetoric of brotherhood and solidarity among peoples, ethnic tensions continued to simmer throughout the Soviet period for a variety of reasons. These included the failure to resolve issues inherited from the Russian Empire, the policy of drawing internal and (to a degree) external borders on the basis of political expediency, and the forced exile of certain ethnic groups from their traditional homelands to Soviet Central Asia and the Soviet Far East.

For many years ethnic grievances could not be openly expressed because in an authoritarian state the personal and collective cost of doing so was heavy and exceeded what most people were willing to pay.[4] The resulting combination of low levels of ethnic protest, official concealment of the protest which did exist, and Soviet claims of ethnic harmony allowed the Soviet state to attribute ethnic conflict to capitalism. The Soviet Union attacked the United States for its exploitation of African-Americans and other minorities while exempting itself from similar charges.[5]

This situation changed when Mikhail Gorbachev came to power in 1985. As First Secretary of the Soviet Communist Party, he simultaneously initiated two seemingly mild reforms whose implications, it appears, he did not fully grasp. First was the policy of perestroika. It called for the slow introduction of market incentives into the Soviet economy. This reform was to serve as the basis for the Soviet Union's entry into the 21st century as a revitalized superpower. The second reform was glasnost. It encouraged individuals, communities, and institutional sectors such as the media and higher education to speak with greater openness on issues that concerned them. These changes, especially glasnost, reduced the risks for challenging established policies, and as a result people began to speak and write more freely. Thus many previously taboo topics were brought out into the open with a breadth and intensity that was unforeseen. Once begun, the process quickly became difficult and then impossible to direct from the top as it assumed a dynamic of its own. In several cases the result has been a series of political and territorial claims and counterclaims that have found expression in violence. Since the last years of the Soviet Union and into the 1990s, the Transcaucasus has been the scene of bitter and violent conflicts between the Georgian government and secessionist movements in Abkhazia and South Ossetia, between the Chechens and Ingush just to the north of the region, and, in the most severe fighting in the region, between Armenians and Azerbaijanis over the disputed enclave of Mountainous Karabagh.[6]

PIERRE VERLUISE AND *ARMÉNIE: LA FRACTURE*

Pierre Verluise is a writer who specializes in Soviet and post-Soviet affairs. He recognized the earthquake and its aftermath as a natural and political event of great importance, and he set himself the modest goal of recording these significant events for the present and future generations. His method was to interview returning French aid workers who were part of one of the largest national rescue teams dispatched to Armenia in early December 1988. Through the words of his informants, he creates a haunting account of the survivors' traumas, the rescuers' attempts to bring some measure of care and comfort, and the political struggles between Gorbachev and the Armenians. A real strength of his study is that he successfully combines issues that are unique and particular to the situation in Armenia and the larger, more universal questions raised by people facing sudden, massive, and irrevocable loss and the slow, painful rebuilding of a shattered world. In this latter sense, his work transcends nationality.

There is yet another sense in which Verluise's effort is important, and to understand that sense, we will have to examine the rarely questioned assumptions that have channeled the way in which Western analysts have looked at the Soviet Union. The academic discipline devoted to the study of the Soviet Union and known as Sovietology was indelibly marked by the collapse of the U.S.–Soviet wartime alliance in 1945. The emergence of the bipolar United States–U.S.S.R. superpower conflict, which defined international relations to such a great degree until the collapse of the Soviet Union in 1991, made Sovietology very much a creature of the Cold War. In other words, Sovietology's growth was linked to the degree in which it could serve Western interests in that struggle.[7]

The Soviet Union was an empire of many peoples that had come into being when its founders seized power in 1917 from the tsars of the Russian Empire. The issue of national minorities loomed large for the early Bolsheviks, who debated the matter intensely. They sought a way of creating a unified Communist state by offering the national minorities sufficient concessions so that they would base their participation on something other than naked force. The compromise solution was to organize internal Soviet borders on an ethnic basis, providing the largest minorities with national homelands within the larger overall context of a centralized Communist, and Russian-dominated, state. The minority republics had many of the trappings of independent states including parliaments, foreign ministries, national flags, anthems, universities, film studios, newspapers and other media, opera houses, athletic teams, ballet troupes, etc. Over the course of time, and especially after World War II, the minority republics began to flex a degree of political muscle as their leadership cadres were increasingly drawn locally. These "national communists" balanced between catering to Moscow's wishes and the desires of the local populations.

By the time Gorbachev came to power in 1985, the minority republics had become significant secondary centers of power within the Soviet system and also the home to problems and issues which Gorbachev and the larger, overall system he directed would not be able to contain, much less satisfy. This became apparent when Gorbachev loosened the reins of control and encouraged more open democratic expression. Gorbachev and the central Party apparatus were soon bedeviled and then overwhelmed by a broad range of protest from all corners of the Soviet Union.

Much of this was missed by Sovietology, and in asking why, we are led to the conclusion that Sovietology was not an ordinary academic discipline but one in the service of power to an inordi-

nate degree. This is not to say that Sovietologists entirely ignored the question of racial and ethnic minorities. The critique is
rather that these topics were marginalized in favor of the study of
an undifferentiated society and its singular political, economic,
and social institutions. The domination of Sovietology by political scientists, with their emphasis on the central governmental
institution and its workings at regional and local levels, helped to
create and then reinforce a perspective that smoothed over any
possible disjuncture between Sovietology as an academic study
and its service to a larger national foreign-policy agenda. As a
result few studies focused on the history and dynamics of peoples
and their communities from the perspective of their own development. The preferred emphasis was on the impact of such
communities on the center. Thus, to a great degree, Soviet minorities were abandoned in favor of an emphasis on the economy, the military, and foreign policy, which allowed the Soviet
Union to be portrayed as a monolithic enemy state.

I am still struck by the fact that as late as 1989 prominent
U.S. Sovietologists were debating whether Eastern Europe or
the Soviet economy would present greater obstacles for Gorbachev's reform agenda. The question of Soviet minorities was
ranked a distant third. This was at a time when nearly one third
of the population of Armenia had taken to the streets in mass
demonstrations, when Armenia and Azerbaijan were in open
conflict over Mountainous Karabagh, when Georgia and the Baltic republics were beginning to speak openly of independence,
and when a host of grievances in the Soviet Central Asian republics were taking on an increasingly ethnic-national— i.e. we ver-
sus the Russians—caste. In point of fact, the issues raised by the
national minorities, including the Armenians, should have been
ranked first along with the economy as the main factors which so
profoundly changed the Soviet Union over the next two years.

The February 1988 Yerevan protests over Mountainous Karabagh moved democratic expression in the Soviet Union to a
new plateau, and Gorbachev's arrest of the Karabagh Committee, which had been leading the struggle for Mountainous Karabagh and coordinating the earthquake relief efforts, revealed the
limits of Soviet reform. These were the local Armenian manifestations of a system-wide tension between centralized control

and growing identity and self-confidence among Soviet minority peoples. The inability either to contain or to resolve minority grievances proved fatal to the system.

In order to understand the last days of the Soviet Union, it is necessary to understand the last days of Soviet Armenia and the other minority republics. Only then can the vast complexities and nuances of social change be grasped. Pierre Verluise's book cannot stand as the whole story, of course, because each republic has its own unique history, but his book does stand as a stark and gripping record of Armenia in the momentous year of 1988. As such, it tells an important part of the story of what happened in Armenia and to the Soviet Union.

THE ARMENIANS

The Armenians are thought to be descended from the ancient Urartians, and they have inhabited the regions of eastern Anatolia and the southern Transcaucasus since well before the time of Christ. References to Armenia and Armenians have been found in Persian rock inscriptions, and Herodotus and Xenophon and other Greeks wrote of them. At the height of their powers in the first century BC, the Armenians under Tigranes the Great forged a short-lived empire that stretched from the Caspian to the Mediterranean Seas. The empire of this period is still recalled as "Sea to Sea Armenia."

In 301 AD, the Armenians converted to Christianity as their state religion, and the Armenian alphabet, still in use, was invented in the early fifth century.

Located at the crossroads of Asia and Europe, Armenia was subject to conquests, first by the Arabs and later by the Persians, Mongols, and Seljuk Turks. The last eastern Armenian kingdom at Ani fell to the Byzantines in 1045 AD and was razed by the Seljuks in 1064. A later Cilician (Anatolian) Armenian kingdom survived until 1375. From that time on until a brief period of independence beginning in 1918, Armenians were a stateless people who relied on their church, language, and literature as vehicles for national identity.

Mountainous Karabagh represented a partial exception to this loss of national independence by virtue of its relatively inaccessible mountainous terrain and remoteness. It long served as a bastion of Armenian national identity and survival during these many centuries, and even during the darkest periods of foreign conquest, Armenian princes managed to exert a degree of authority in the region.[8] These princely families in Mountainous Karabagh survived until the Russian conquest in the early nineteenth century.

Beginning in the mid-nineteenth century Armenians underwent a national revival that incorporated literary/cultural and political dimensions.[9] Members of the Armenian intelligentsia grappled with the problem of a nation divided between the Russian and Ottoman Turkish Empires.

This period of growing Armenian national consciousness on both sides of the Russian–Turkish frontier coincided with the decline of the Ottoman Empire, which included its earlier loss of Greece and its defeats in the Balkans. At the same time Armenians in the eastern provinces of Anatolia found their position eroded by the more rapidly increasing Turkish and Kurdish populations and the settlement of Moslems from the Balkans and the North Caucasus. In the latter region, resistance to the southward Russian advance was broken during this period.

During the years 1894–1896, Anatolian Armenians were massacred on the order of Ottoman Sultan Abdul Hamid and 200,000 perished. Many leading Armenian political activists allied themselves with the Young Turk reform movement in the belief that the overthrow of the Sultanate and its replacement by a constitutional form of government offered the best hope for Ottoman minorities. The Sultanate was overthrown in 1908 amid great rejoicing by Turks, Armenians, and other Ottoman minorities, but Armenian hopes were cruelly dashed with the ascension to power of the most nationalistic elements of the Young Turk movement, which brought the Ottoman Empire into World War I as an ally of Germany and Austria–Hungry. In 1915, under the cover of war, the Ottoman Turkish rulers unleashed a policy of genocide against the Armenians. Three hundred thousand Armenians fled across the border to Russian Armenia. Adult males who could not escape were killed while women and children were driven in forced marches to the de-

serts of northern Syria. Estimates of Armenian deaths range
from 600,000 to over 2 million during this period from the
1915 massacres to subsequent and related events continuing to
1923.[10]

In the post-war peace settlement, two separate treaties were
negotiated between the Entente and Turkey, the successor state
to the defeated Ottoman Empire. The Treaty of Sèvres called for
the creation of an independent Armenian state in the Caucasus
and eastern Anatolia, as well as Palestinian and Kurdish states
elsewhere. This treaty was stillborn because of the military successes of the Turkish nationalist movement organized by Mustafa
Kemal (Atatürk). Atatürk's victories allowed Turkey to bargain
from a position of strength, and the result was the reopening of
the treaty negotiations. In the second treaty, the Treaty of
Lausanne, Armenia and Armenians were never mentioned. The
only territorial Armenia was the independent republic in the
Transcaucasus, which the Armenians had proclaimed in May
1918. This republic was soon under siege by the Kemalists and
the Bolsheviks. It fell to the latter at the end of 1920 with part of
its lands (Kars and Ardahan) ceded to Turkey.

Independent Armenia had been landlocked and the home to
a large and destitute refugee population. Compared to Georgia
and Azerbaijan, Armenia was the weakest and least viable of the
three independent Transcaucasian states. Edmund M. Herzig
has recently written that "Armenia in 1920 was a devastated and
desperate land—the post-First World War equivalent of today's
Ethiopia or Sudan." [11]

The Bolshevik revolution was itself in doubt during these
years. The Bolsheviks were challenged both by invading armies
from the West and Japan and by indigenous counterrevolution-
ary forces. For Lenin, the first priority was the defense of the
revolution and not issues of self-determination for minority peoples. The Armenians, bargaining from a weak position, had their
interests sacrificed to the larger Bolshevik concern with securing
the safety of the revolution. This was the context in which
Lenin and Atatürk came to agree that the Bolsheviks would
have secure borders in the Transcaucasus in return for three
territorial concessions to Turkey, all of them at the expense of
the Armenians. The regions of Kars and Ardahan, which had

been part of the independent Armenian Republic, went to Turkey, while Nakhichevan and Mountainous Karabagh were ceded to Turkey's ally, Azerbaijan.

Decades later when the Armenian protests over Mountainous Karabagh became international news in February 1988, the region was described as "obscure." Indeed, it was scarcely known in the West, and few elsewhere in the Soviet Union could identify it. There were even Armenians in the Armenian S.S.R. who had little information about this nearby region still populated by a substantial Armenian majority. Nevertheless, the impact of this territory (which is slightly larger than Rhode Island) on Armenia, Azerbaijan, and the Soviet Union can scarcely be overestimated.

In the summer and fall of 1987 Armenia saw the beginnings of organized public protest. The issues were pollution, widespread corruption, the slow pace of reform, and a nuclear power plant not far from the capital city. Activists pointed out that Medzamor was a replica of the ill-fated Chernobyl plant in the Ukraine and charged that the facility had been sited on an earthquake fault. None of these protests drew more than a few thousand people.

This changed dramatically a few months later. Armenians in Mountainous Karabagh began their protests in January and February of 1988. In February the region's Supreme Soviet called upon the Supreme Soviet of the U.S.S.R. to transfer the territory to Armenia. Very soon thereafter Armenians in Yerevan took to the streets by the hundreds of thousands for marches, demonstrations, and rallies in support of this demand. Nora Dudwick, an anthropologist from the University of Pennsylvania, was an eyewitness to these events, and she recorded the exhilaration and shared feelings of transcendence among the participants. An Armenian journalist speaking with Dudwick of an all-night 30-kilometer march through Yerevan captures the mood:

> It was an unforgettable night, very moving. The mood was radiant, lofty, calm. People marched without feeling tired . . . we forgot about our injuries and impotence.[12]

Another participant noted that, "In these days, as if in one leap, we came to a new level of humanity." [13]

One of the most striking features of these demonstrations was that the Yerevan rallies in support of striking Armenians in Mountainous Karabagh began with a 5,000 person demonstration on a Saturday and escalated into a half a million people, in effect, a general strike within a few days. Dudwick argues persuasively that Mountainous Karabagh struck a responsive chord in Armenians that brought them together, providing unity in a way that other concerns could not. She quotes a schoolteacher who explained:

> Pollution touches people physically but is more difficult to internalize. Karabagh, on the other hand, strikes at the core of our collective essence. [14]

At the core of the "collective essence" stands the 1915 genocide, the deaths of a million people, and the loss of Turkish Armenia, Nakhichevan, and Mountainous Karabagh. Dudwick captures the collective meaning of past events for the Armenian people:

> Armenians had the experience of feeling themselves united as a people, of feeling the barriers of structure temporarily dissolve, of remembering their common humanity, history, and destiny. Perhaps we can consider the Karabagh movement as a national *rite de passage* which is transforming Karabagh from a symbol of past glories and past losses into a symbol of the Armenian's ability to wage a sustained struggle for the reappropriation of their own past, present, and future. [15]

The Karabagh protests brought the issue of national minorities in the Soviet Union further to the fore. There had been earlier protests by the Crimean Tatars and mass-based protests and government repression in Kazakhstan's capital city of Alma-Ata in December 1986, but nothing had the electrifying effect of Mountainous Karabagh. Other nationalities were emboldened by the protests. The Baltic republics, for example, had largely employed low-key consciousness-raising methods such as traditional folk festivals and had pursued legalistic, constitutional means to press their claims for independence. In the wake of Mountainous Karabagh, Baltic nationalists began organizing more visible, larger-scale mass protests that contributed to their declaration of independence after the failed August 1991 coup.

In Armenia, the Karabagh Organizing Committee was assembled to give direction to the protests. In December 1988 the Committee took over the Armenian earthquake relief efforts only to have Gorbachev cynically employ the distraction of the earthquake to order the Committee members arrested. They were held in Moscow for six months and released in May 1989 without trial. These arrests backfired on Gorbachev. The Committee members' status as national heroes among Armenians was strengthened, while the standing of Gorbachev and the Armenian and Soviet Communist parties hit new lows from which they would not recover.

The die was now cast. What had begun as a massive natural catastrophe had become quickly politicized. The arrests, the ineptness of the official Communist relief efforts, corruption in the distribution of relief supplies, and Gorbachev's refusal to act on Mountainous Karabagh radically alienated the Armenians and set them firmly on the path to national independence. Whatever solutions there would be to the issues of earthquake reconstruction and Mountainous Karabagh now lay within that ambiguous future.

NOTES

1. For Armenia, see Richard Hovannisian, *Armenia on the Road to Independence* (Los Angeles, 1967) and *The Republic of Armenia*, vols. I and II (Los Angeles, 1971 and 1982); for Georgia, Ronald Grigor Suny, *The Making of the Georgian Nation* (Bloomington, Indiana, 1988); and for Azerbaijan, Tadeusz Swietochowski, *Russian Azerbaijan, 1905–1920* (Cambridge, UK, 1985).

2. For a superb discussion of these themes see Ronald Suny, "The Revenge of the Past: Socialism and Ethnic Conflict in Transcaucasia," *New Left Review*, no. 184 (October/November, 1990), pp. 5–34. For the British role consult Akaby Nassibian, *Britain and the Armenian Question, 1915–1923* (London, 1984).

3. Suny, "Revenge," op. cit.

4. Thorough discussions of Soviet dissent may be found in Ludmilla Al-

exeyeva, *Soviet Dissent: Contemporary Movements for National, Religious, and Human Rights* (Middletown, Connecticut, 1985) and Yaroslav Bilinsky and Tonu Parming, *Helsinki Watch Committees in the Soviet Union: Implications for the Soviet Nationality Question* (n.p.: Final Report for the National Council for Soviet and Eastern European Research, 1980).

5. A Soviet assessment of Soviet nationality policy may be found in E. Bagramov, *The CPSU's Nationalities Policy* (Moscow, 1988).

6. See Julian Birch, "Border Disputes and Disputed Borders in the Soviet Federated System," *Nationalities Papers*, XV (1987), pp. 47–58 for a discussion of some of the disputed territories within the Soviet Union. The conflict over Mountainous Karabagh ranks second in deadliness after the violence in the former Soviet Central Asian republic of Tajikistan where deaths are reported to exceed 40,000.

7. Alexander J. Motyl, *Sovietology, Rationality, Nationality: Coming to Grips with Nationalism in the USSR* (New York, 1990), chapter 1 and Ian Bremmer and Ray Taras, eds., *Nation and Politics in Soviet Successor States* (Cambridge, 1993), pp. 11–12.

8. Robert Hewson, "The Meliks of Eastern Armenia," *Revue des Etudes Arméniennes*, part I, vol. IX (1972); part II, vol. X (1973/1974); and part IV, vol. XIV (1980).

9. Louise Nalbandian, *The Armenian Revolutionary Movement: The Development of Armenian Political Parties through the Nineteenth Century* (Los Angeles, 1963).

10. Turkey continues to deny that a genocide was committed, and has attempted to conceal and alter the historical record both for its own people and the larger world community. Because of Turkey's strategic location in the Cold War struggle and its membership in NATO dating from the early 1950s, Turcophile histories of the World War I period have received an increasingly sympathetic hearing in the United States, and Turkey has requested and received support (bipartisan support) from the U.S. government in Congress and in international forums such as the United Nations when the issue of the Armenian genocide has been raised. For documentation of the genocide see Richard Hovannisian, *The Armenian Holocaust: A Bibliography Relating to the Deportations, Massacres, and Dispersion of the Armenian People, 1915–1923* (Cambridge, Massachusetts, 1978); Permanent People's Tribunal, *A Crime of Silence: The Armenian Genocide* (London, 1985); Vahakn Dadrian, "The Naim-Andonian Documents on the World War I Destruction of Ottoman Armenians: The Anatomy of a Genocide," *International Journal of Middle East Studies*, vol. 18 (1986), pp. 311–360; Vahakn Dadrian, "Genocide as a Problem of National and International Law: The World War I Armenian Case and Its Contemporary Legal Ramifications," *Yale Journal of International Law*, vol. 14, no. 2, (1989), pp. 221–334; Leslie A. Davis, *The Slaughterhouse Province: An American Diplomat's Report on the Armenian Genocide, 1915–1917* (New Rochelle, New York, 1989); Donald E. Miller and Lorna Touryan Miller, *Survivors: An Oral History of the Armenian Genocide* (Berkeley and Los Angeles, 1993); and Raymond H. Kevorkian and Paul B. Paboudjian, *Les Arméniens dans l'Empire ottoman à la veille du génocide* (Paris, 1992). For a fascinating analysis of recent attempts at genocide denial by the Turkish state apparatus, see Roger W. Smith, Eric Markusen, and Robert Jay Lifton, "Professional Ethics and the Denial of the Armenian Genocide," *Holocaust and Genocide Studies*, vol. 9, no. 1 (1995), pp. 1–22.

11. Edmund M. Herzig, "Armenians," in Graham Smith, ed., *The Nationalities Question in the Soviet Union* (London and New York, 1990), p. 148.

12. Nora Dudwick, "The Karabagh Movement: An Old Scenario Gets Rewritten," *The Armenian Review*, vol. 42 (1989), p. 67. For an analysis of the Armenians'

use of symbols of protest, see Stephanie Platz, "The Karabagh Demonstrations: Visual Representations of Armenian Identity," *The Annual of the Society for the Study of Caucasia*, 3 (1991), pp. 19–30.

13. Ibid., p. 67.

14. Nora Dudwick, "Moments That Will Live Forever: The First Year of the Karabagh Movement," presented at the Karabagh/Artsakh Conference, Columbia University, New York, 11 February 1989, p. 4.

15. Ibid., p. 9.

Abbreviations

Pierre Verluise uses a number of acronyms to refer to French public and private organizations involved in the disaster relief effort. The acronyms and their English equivalents are provided here for the reader's convenience.

CNRS
: National Center for Scientific Research. This organization brings together university researchers and is linked to the Ministry of National Education.

COLMED 16
: Medical unit comprised of doctors, rescue workers, and an emergency field unit. A branch of Public Safety.

COSI
: Standing Committee for International Aid. A private sector organization.

COTAM
: Military Air Transport Command. Attached to the Ministry of Defense.

DACO
: Advanced Detachment for Operational Coordination. A branch of Public Safety working with DICA units.

DAM 30
: Medical Support Detachment for the Department of Gard (No. 30). A branch of Public Safety.

DICA
: Air Detachment for Disaster Intervention. A branch of Public Safety consisting of men, dog teams, medical personnel, and six tons of rescue and first-aid equipment. It can be assembled in three hours.

DWB
: Doctors without Borders. An international medical organization based in France; founded in 1971. It responds to medical crises caused by wars and natural disasters around the world.

ORSEC Plan created in 1957 to respond to natural disasters and civil disorders. The plan makes all necessary public and private emergency response resources available to local governments.

SAMU An emergency medical response organization based in the Ministry of Health. It is organized at the local level and works out of hospital units.

UMAF Union of Armenian Physicians of France. A private organization incorporated in 1901.

USIIC Public Safety Training and Intervention Unit. Military intervention units organized by the central government.

Political Map of the Caucasus (1988)

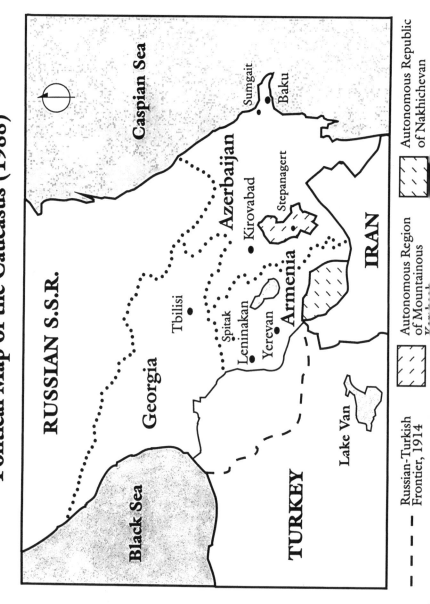

RUSSIAN S.S.R.

Caspian Sea

Sumgait

Baku

Azerbaijan

Kirovabad

Stepanagert

Tbilisi

Georgia

Spitak

Leninakan

Yerevan

Armenia

IRAN

Black Sea

Lake Van

TURKEY

- - - Russian-Turkish
Frontier, 1914

Autonomous Region
of Mountainous
Karabakh

Autonomous Republic
of Nakhichevan

Armenia
IN CRISIS
THE 1988
EARTHQUAKE

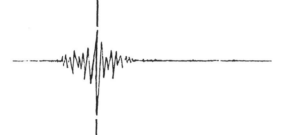

Foreword

GÉRARD CHALIAND

The earthquake that hit Armenia on 7 December 1988 reverberated throughout the world. Never before, perhaps, had a natural disaster brought forth international aid of such significance and solidarity on such a scale.

Above all, this disaster affected the Soviet Union of Gorbachev, and for the first time in their history, Soviet authorities allowed foreigners to bring aid to their disaster victims. Operation Armenia was a first, and for this reason of interest to the West. Government agencies and private organizations specializing in disaster relief left immediately. Among them were (first and foremost) France, and thanks to the diligent efforts of Secretary of State Bernard Kouchner organizations such as Physicians for the World, Doctors without Borders (recognized by all for its efficiency), and Handicap International, followed by Switzerland with Caritas, the United States, Canada, Great Britain, West Germany, the Scandinavian countries, Japan, an Israeli mission led by General Vardi, etc.

However, the fact that the earthquake occurred in the U.S.S.R. and that the Soviet Union allowed foreign assistance is not the only reason for the extraordinary worldwide interest in the disaster, though it is the main one. There are three other factors:

1. Since February of 1988 there had been more or less per-

manent demonstrations in Yerevan involving hundreds of thousands of people. The dual demands of the protestors were expressed by the Karabagh Committee, which operated outside of the official institutional structure: democratization and the reunification of Armenia and the autonomous region of Mountainous Karabagh, which has an Armenian majority of 80 percent. A series of ecological demands were grafted onto these: closure of the Medzamor nuclear power plant, closure of the heavily polluting chemical plant at Nairit, etc. Along with the political claims of the Estonians—who toned down their ethnic problems insofar as they concerned only the Russians and not other populations in the empire—the Armenian claims were the first, the largest in scale, and perhaps the most peaceful and resolute in the Soviet Union.

2. For fifteen years, national and public opinion was focused on the mass deportation and liquidation of Anatolian Armenians (1915–1916). This deportation was ordered by the Young Turks after the group-by-group disarming and liquidation of Armenian military recruits and the arrest on 24 April 1915 and the nearly total liquidation of some six hundred Armenian intellectuals and public figures in Constantinople. As for the deportation orders, they were to be carried out only in the border areas along the Caucasus; however, they were put into effect throughout the whole of eastern Anatolia to the Syrian border. Only the urban communities of Constantinople and Smyrna were spared.

Of the Armenian population of Anatolia, 40 to 50 percent was liquidated en route.[1] With a persistence deserving a better cause then this one, the Turkish state continues to deny these organized massacres, which we call genocide today. (What is the credibility of a state that has officially denied for half a century the existence of a Kurdish minority on Turkish territory generally estimated at between eight and ten million persons?) Patient efforts led by the Armenian diaspora have allowed the world to learn of these events, and international bodies—including the United Nations Sub-Commission on Human Rights and the Council of Europe—have officially recognized the genocide.

The earthquake took place after a dozen years of debate in the West over the question of the Armenian genocide and after ten months of political unrest in Armenia. In a certain way, the outpouring of sympathy and aid was the outcome of a lengthy maturation of the "Armenian question."

3. Finally, it cannot be denied that the Armenians of the U.S.S.R. benefited simultaneously from Gorbachev's glasnost policies, political work that concerned problems specific to Armenians, and the objective reality which allowed the West to identify easily with them. Western public opinion is not always ready to extend such a burst of solidarity to non-whites when they do not serve the political interests of the West. However, the flow of sympathy with regard to the students of Peking and the Chinese demonstrators represents an advance in this respect. Tragic though it may be, the earthquake and its impact in the media brought Armenians and Armenia back into the mainstream from the rumors of history, that they had been put to fire and sword between 1915 and 1920. As is well known, in a hostile environment small nations pay more dearly than others for the right to survive and to be heard.

Along with demands for democratization, which are the foundation of the politics of the Karabagh Committee, the Committee also demands (with the unanimous approval of the Armenian people) the unification of Mountainous Karabagh. The adminstration of this region was conferred upon Azerbaijan by the central government in 1921—at the same time as Nakhichevan, which by now has been emptied of its Armenian population.

The Committee's claim is legitimate, since self-determination rests upon the will of the people. In this regard, the refusal to yield to Armenian demands reveals the limits and ambiguities of glasnost: consider the arrest of eleven members of the Committee followed by their release without trial (this was publicly supported by Andrei Sakharov, among others), and the transfer of the administration of Mountainous Karabagh from Baku to Moscow. Yet nothing has been resolved. Moscow must manage a situation in which it does not seem possible to wear down Armenian claims to Mountainous Karabagh. At the same time, how can they not alienate the Azerbaijanis who are not indifferent to Shi'ite propaganda from Iran (the Azerbaijanis are Shi'ite and speak Turkish) and who do not lack for ties with Turkey?

What has occurred was forseeable, given the ethno-religious antagonisms between Armenians and Azerbaijanis, which was reinforced by Azerbaijani massacres of Armenians in Baku and Shushi in 1905 and the elimination of tens of Azerbaijani villages by Armenian troops in 1918. The Sumgait pogroms in Azerbaijan (1988) remind us that these practices have not come to an end. Seventy years of terror and the habit of terror have held back the expression of conflict without eliminating any of the sources. It is not surprising that the process of evolution, as it allows political and/or social grievances to be expressed, can cause ethnic or ethno-religious antagonisms to explode.[2]

We see demands for sovereignty in the Baltic states and Moldavia where Russification in the demographic sense is so sensitive. Elsewhere, in Kazakhstan, where Russification is well advanced, reactions did not even wait for the development of glasnost.

The struggle for Mountainous Karabagh and the right to democracy is not over, and it is difficult to see a way out. Moreover, there is little chance that Moscow will accede to Armenian demands for fear of Azerbaijani reactions. Nevertheless, the directors of the Karabagh Committee exhibit a great deal of political maturity by remaining within the Union and furthering democratization and self-determination for the population of Mountainous Karabagh.

Bloody confrontations are forseeable, since relations between Christians and Moslems from the Balkans to the Caucasus are based on mutual rejection. Gorbachev is caught between the problems of economics and nationality; given the weakness of his social base, he risks becoming the victim of still unexpressed popular anger from which the conservative bureaucracy will profit.

This book about the 7 December 1988 Armenian earthquake and the conditions surrounding it is at once thoughtful and thorough. Pierre Verluise has produced a model contemporary history with the necessary restraint, without exaggerating an event sufficiently dramatic to maintain its full impact when simply reported and analyzed. This is a serious investigator who spoke with dozens of witnesses in the days after the earthquake: physicians, nurses, earthquake specialists, and the like. The information has been verified and corroborated; this solidly documented book reveals many aspects of the drama that were not reported in the French press at the time. Going beyond a simple event-by-event reportage, Pierre Verluise has tried to bring out a historic perspective that presents the earthquake in all its dimensions.

Those who were best prepared to deal with this tragedy were organizations with a long history of experience in dealing with conditions in underdeveloped countries, especially those such as Doctors without Borders, which have a tradition of independent intervention.

Finally this book is a tribute to the courage and dignity of the victims and the reassuring solidarity that was expressed in December of 1988 and which continues. The Armenians are not alone.

NOTES

1. This proportion remains true whatever the calculations may be of the Armenian population (varying between 1.5 and 2 million on the eve of World War I). The number of victims varies between 600,000 (lower estimate of J. McCarthy, see bibliography) and 1.1 million (upper estimate of J. Lepsius).

2. In March 1989 Turkmens attacked Armenian cooperatives and restaurants in Ashkhabad (capital of Turkmenistan). [*Translator's note:* Since 1989 and into the post-Soviet period there have been serious ethnic clashes elsewhere in Central Asia, in Georgia, and in Moldavia as well as between Armenians and Azerbaijanis.]

Preface

PIERRE VERLUISE

Why should I, a non-Armenian, plan a work devoted to the earthquake that devastated Armenia on 7 December 1988?

THE IDEA

Around 15 December 1988 I had the idea of meeting the first rescue workers returning from Armenia. My original intention was to analyze the response of the Soviet system to a crisis situation, since such moments are often revealing. Convinced that the tragedy had to be recorded and recognized in order for there to be a proper mourning, a second motivation was quickly added: to preserve the memory of a major historical event. But how would this contribution see the light of day?

THE METHOD

In order to maintain the objectivity necessary to work on a tragedy of this magnitude, I decided not to proceed until relief efforts were well underway in the disaster areas. I also decided to meet with a large number of relief workers. Since I was not directly involved in the drama, I was in a position to collect extraordinary eyewitness accounts. Most of the witnesses I met with went to Armenia with Médecins sans Frontières (hereafter Doctors without Borders, or DWB).[1] I met with them individually after they had participated in the same collective relief activities. This allowed me to verify information from a number of sources who had dealt with the same problems and developed a similar perspective and point of view.

The events reported here cover the period from 7 December 1988, the date of the earthquake, to 7 January 1989, the date of the arrest of all of the members of the Karabagh Committee. The human dimensions of the disaster are the subject of the first four chapters; the last two chapters present the larger historical and political context.

ACKNOWLEDGMENTS

This book would not have been possible without the collaboration of numerous people. First I wish to thank Saphia Méchery (Director of Public Relations, Doctors without Borders) who was the first to express an interest in this project and Rony Brauman (President, Doctors without Borders) who honored me with his trust and provided the means to carry out this investigation. Beyond the president himself, I express my sincere gratitude to Doctors without Borders. Next I have the pleasure of thanking the 31 witnesses who agreed to meet with me after their return from Armenia:

— Gérard Bekmezian (physician, went to Armenia with DWB);

— Gérard Bollini (physician, professor of pediatric surgery, member of DWB, who left on a cargo plane provided by the city of Marseilles);

— Lieutenant Colonel Caillarec (Chief of Staff, Public Safety, French detachment);

— Elizabeth Caniot (nephrologist, DWB);

— Yves Carbonnel (dialysis technician, DWB);

— Chief Physician Chevalier (Chief of the French detachment in Armenia);

— Thierry Clima (logistical coordinator, DWB);

— Carl Cordonnier (logistical coordinator, photographer, DWB);

— Antoine Crouan (physician, communications director, DWB);

— Georges Dallemagne (mission coordinator, DWB, Yerevan);

— Ara Dandiguian (physician, DWB);

— Franck David (hygienist, DWB);

— Victor E. Davidovici (seismic engineering adviser, scientific mission in Armenia);

— Jean-Michel Ekhérian (anesthesiologist, DWB);

— Xavier Emmanuelli (physician, vice president of DWB);

— Olivier Fournier (anesthesiologist, DWB);

— Aram Gazarian (surgical intern, DWB);

— Maurice Gazarian (businessman, accompanied two cargo planes sent by SOS/Armenia);

— Jean Gulian (physician with a specialty in the biological sciences, DWB);

— Gérard Hovakimian (physician, DWB);

— Viken Kazandjian (pediatric surgeon, DWB);

— Georges Képénékian (urological surgeon);

— Frédéric Khidichian (psychiatric intern, DWB/UMAF);

— Annie Koulaksezian (physician, COSI);

— Christian Levaux (logistical coordinator, DWB);

— Pierre Mouroux (engineer ECP, Bureau of Geological and Mineral Research, Seismic Risk and Engineering Service, scientific mission in Armenia);

— Pierre-Marie Sarant (emergency director at DWB, coordinator of the DWB mission in Leninakan);

— Serge Simonian (surgeon, founder of UMAF, treasurer of SOS/Armenia, UMAF/SOS-Armenia);

— Rolande Sprache (nurse, DWB);

— Aram Ter Minassian (anesthesiologist, SAMU 94, French detachment in Armenia);

— Yves Ternon (surgeon, historian specializing in the Armenian genocide, DWB);

For their cooperation I also thank the four following people who participated in the organization of relief aid in France:

— Lieutenant Colonel Leblanc (Director of Central Operations for Public Safety);

— Véronique Falque (nephrologist, Secretary General of DWB, responsible for the coordination of Operation Hemodialysis in Marseilles);

— Brigitte Vasset (physician, responsible for DWB missions and the Armenian mission for the three weeks following the earthquake);

— Jacques Pinal (pharmacist, director of operations, director of logistics for DWB).

I thank Levon Ter Petrossian, member of the Karabagh Committee for his trust during our meeting on 25 July 1989. I also express my deepest gratitude to four specialists on Armenia and the Soviet Union who helped me to put together the third part of this book devoted to the political dimensions of these events:

— Karen Agoulian;

— Claire Mouradian (Chief of Research at CNRS);

— Anahide Ter Minassian (Senior Lecturer at the University of Paris I);

— Françoise Thom (Research Attaché at the French Institute of Military Studies).

Transcribing the large number of taped interviews that make up the basis for this work was carried out with great competence by Christine Constant, Véronique Gaillard, Lydia Goubet, Christine Lamiche, and Odile Hardy. The last-named was also in charge of typing the manuscript. I thank them for their efficiency, which allowed me to meet a tight publication schedule.

Finally, my fullest gratitude goes to those who offered me their suggestions after reading all or part of the manuscript: Jeannine Blanchet, Gérard Chaliand, Jean-Michel Ekhérian, Véronique Falque, Marc Gastellu Etchegorry, Georges Képénékian, Claude Mutafian, Anahide Ter Minassian, Aram Ter Minassian, Levon Ter Petrossian, Yves Ternon, and François and Jeannie Verluise.

Of course, I accept full responsibility for the findings of this investigation.

I extend my warmest affection to my wife Sylvie and our son Tanguy who had to endure long months of "absences" due to the demands imposed by this book.

POSTSCRIPT

I extend my deepest gratitude to Professor Levon Chorbajian who undertook the English translation of *Arménie: La Fracture* on his own initiative and thus gave my work a second life. I thank Anne-Michéle Chaumeton for her capable work in assisting me with the final editing of the English language edition. And I also want to thank Mr. Arthur Evans, director of Wayne State University Press, for his support in publishing the English-language edition.

NOTES

1. Doctors without Borders, 8 rue Saint-Sabin, 75011 Paris, France. Tel.: (1) 40–21–29–29.

PART I

A
MAJOR
CATASTROPHE

CHAPTER 1

The Earthquake
and Initial
Relief Efforts

Wednesday, 7 December 1988 from 11:41 to 11:45 a.m., the Armenian earth trembled.

Tens of thousands of men, women, and children perished within moments, crushed under the debris of buildings ill-suited to resist the earthquake.

In the following days, several thousand others injured at the time of the earthquake died. Despite their best efforts, Soviet and foreign rescue workers were not able to dig out more than 80 survivors from the rubble.

This ordeal will leave its mark for a long time on the 500,000 to 700,000 victims as well as the 6 million Armenians living in the Soviet Union and in the diaspora.

This earthquake was unique in three respects. It struck a people still haunted by the genocide committed against it at the beginning of this century. The killings, carried out in 1915 by the Young Turk government against nearly half of the Armenian people, remains engraved in their memory. "Two catastrophes of such a scale in less than a century for such a small nation, it is too much," confided one of the Armenian witnesses in summarizing public feeling.[1]

Second, the cataclysm took place at the worst possible moment, in the midst of a political conflict between the Armenians and the Soviet system.

Finally, in the days following the earthquake, the Soviet authorities sought to reassert political control. Briefly, let us recall the historic context in which nature itself played such a great role.

This earthquake followed fifteen months of political agitation, during which the Soviet powers attempted to reclaim their authority.

Triggered in the summer of 1987 by an alarmist article concerned with ecological degradation in Armenia and signed by a member of the Communist Party, the opposition movement started action on 1 September 1987. At that time, the large majority of Armenians had confidence that Mr. Gorbachev would respond to their concerns. Only a minority made a claim to democracy. Into this turmoil the longstanding aspiration for the reunification of Mountainous Karabagh—an enclave populated by an Armenian majority but administered by Azerbaijani authorities—with the Armenian Republic asserted itself once again. Several members of the Communist Party declared themselves in favor of this claim, and the Armenians believed that they would be understood in high places.

On 18 February 1988, there was bitter disappointment: a delegation returned to Yerevan empty-handed after having tried in vain to defend Armenian aspirations in Moscow. Over a week of demonstrations followed, during which the Karabagh Committee took its initial form.

On 26 February 1988, Mr. Gorbachev asked for one month to consider the problem. Still confident, the Armenians suspended their demonstrations.

On 28 and 29 February 1988, the Azerbaijanis murdered several dozen Armenians at Sumgait, causing profound distress in the Armenian community. More and more Armenians questioned Gorbachev's willingness to defend their interests while continuing to hope that justice would be done. The national movement, embodied by the Karabagh Committee and backed by nearly all of the people, assumed responsibility for helping the refugees from Sumgait.

On 25 March 1988, at the end of the one-month moratorium, Gorbachev failed to put forth any substantial political compromise. This only widened the breach that had been developing between the Soviet state and the Armenians for some time, since those responsible for the Sumgait murders remained unpunished.

During the following months, democratic aspirations continued to grow. Relations between the Communist authorities and the people worsened. Armenian society now recognized as its sole legitimate representative the Karabagh Committee as it had evolved with the eleven following members: Levon Ter Petrossian, Alexane Hakobian, Babken Ararktsian, Vano Siradeghian, Vazguen Manoukian, Raphael Ghazarian, Hambardzoum Galoustian, Davit Vardanian, Achot Manoutcharian, Samson Ghazarian, and Samuel Guevorguian.

This evolution culminated on 7 November 1988, on the occasion of the anniversary of the 1917 Revolution. One million Armenians invaded Lenin Square where the ceremonies were unfolding, booing Party representatives and not leaving their places until word came from the Committee members.

After this humiliation, the Party augmented its pressure, declaring a state of emergency on 24 November 1988 and instituting a curfew from 8 p.m. to 6 a.m.[2] On 28 November 1988 the Soviet authorities arrested Sergei Grigoryants, editor and chief of the independent journal *Glasnost*, who had come to investigate, and sentenced him to thirty days in prison.

Martial law failed to settle the ethnic conflict between the Azerbaijanis and the Armenians. According to the press director of the Ministry of Interior, Mr. Mikhailov, "On the one morning of 30 November 1988," 7,800 Armenian refugees arrived in Armenia from Azerbaijan.[3] Since the Sumgait massacres, 100,000 Armenians had fled their homes. These new arrivals increased the number of earthquake victims.

Noting the conflictual situation, tourists returning from Armenia confided, "Anything is possible, anything can happen." Yet no one could have imagined that the Armenian earth would tremble.

THE EARTHQUAKE AND THE FIRST RELIEF EFFORTS

Wednesday, 7 December 1988 at 11:41 a.m., at a time when families were most spread out—men at work, children at school, women with the youngest ones at home—the land shook for the first time.

Martin Pachaian, a teacher in Leninakan, remembers:

I was giving a French lesson to my students in the third grade. I was reading them a poem by Eluard entitled "A Smile." I scarcely had time to read this very beautiful line which says, "At the end of every sorrow is always an open window," when we had the first jolt. The cupboard which was behind me turned over. I had time to pick myself up and tell the students, "Don't be afraid, get out." Then the walls moved apart. I slipped and fell.[4]

At 11:45 a second tremor brought the world to an end. The majority of students in this school perished along with the wife and two children of this teacher.

After wandering for several days among the ruins, he would be the translator for the Doctors without Borders (DWB) rescue team now in Leninakan.

The earthquake struck a region of the republic made up of the cities of Spitak, Leninakan, Kirovakan, Stepanavan, and about fifty villages. At the end of the second part of this chapter we will present an estimate of the destruction and human loss.

In the minutes following the catastrophe, the very large majority of survivors were in a daze. Then several "natural leaders," who were soon joined by other survivors, began to unearth the most accessible of the injured.

Unfortunately, these first efforts to give assistance were not very effective. They were carried out by a population directly involved in the drama, possessing little knowledge and few medical personnel, two-thirds of the latter having disappeared among the rubble of the medical facilities.

There was a clear and urgent need for competent aid from the outside. But who would bring help to the victims?

Until Friday, 9 December at 9:15 p.m., the time of arrival of a French rescue team, the victims received help from nearby areas, from Yerevan, then Georgia, and Mountainous Karabagh. The Soviet army, ever present, did not take part in the search for victims, not even to light up the ruins at night with the headlights from their vehicles, thereby reducing the possibility of rescuing survivors after dark.

The Karabagh Committee in Action

Confronted with the initially poorly organized state of relief efforts, the Karabagh Committee set aside its political concerns to take charge of estimating destruction, the human loss, and the pressing needs of the victims as well as coordinating relief from abroad.

Bernard Guetta wrote in *Le Monde* on 7 December:

> At a time when Moscow was only thinking about organizing help, it was the Karabagh Committee which organized the initial collections of clothes, blankets, food, and money, and dispatched the first columns of volunteers.

The Armenian people came to the same conclusion. "From the start of the first relief efforts, the Committee was the most logical and efficient in providing medicines and food," related a witness.

We can therefore give credit to Achot Manoutcharian for a text he wrote on 18 December 1988 while still underground. Transmitted to its Paris bureau by the independent journal *Glasnost* on 21 December, it was published in the newspaper *Gamk* on 29 December 1988. First of all, says this Committee member, "Practically all the members of the Karabagh Committee of Armenia left on 7 December for the earthquake sites." After having made an estimate of the losses and needs, they returned at the end of the day to Yerevan and informed L'Agence France Presse of their estimate: 100,000 dead.

> The night of 7 December, at the Writers' Union, a staff office headed by the leaders of our movement was created to coordinate relief efforts. We saw ourselves then as a force for complementing the governmental commission. We contacted them and reached an agreement about our activities. By Thursday evening, 8 December, it was already clear that there could be no question of any centralized relief organization. To the natural difficulties of directing operations, linked with the exceptional character of the situation, we had to add the flagrant incompetence of a large number of leading officials. In this situation, the staff created by the Committee assumed the following tasks:
>
> 1. To create staff offices in Spitak and Leninakan, with representatives in the rural areas, charged with collecting information and coordinating operations. The overwhelming majority of Committee members and grassroots militants worked in these on-site staff offices.
>
> 2. To form volunteer teams supplied with technical equipment, instruments, water reserves, food, clothes, and medicine for the victims. As early as the night of Wednesday, 7 December, we began sending a minimum of sixty to seventy buses of volunteers to the earthquake zones every day.

Indeed, a witness confirms that on the night of 7 December the Committee sent 2,000 relief workers to the victimized areas. "Many volunteers," added A. Manoutcharian, "went to the damaged villages in the Spitak and Akhourian districts, which were totally ignored by the authorities."

3. To evacuate the homeless from the earthquake zones and send them on to families extending their hospitality. Thousands of people signed up at the Writers's Union to welcome victims and waited there, night and day taking survivors with them as they arrived. Nearly everyone wanted to adopt orphans.

4. To explain the situation rationally, on account of the multitude of rumors that circulated and worried people, and to answer people's questions. Given that all the relief teams brought back information from the stricken areas as well as the needs of the staff offices, the Committee had the most reliable information at its disposal concerning the specific needs of different locations. We reached an agreement with the governmental commission so that one of our representatives would be present at the airport and could indicate where the cargo arrivals should be sent.

A relief worker from a French detachment arriving Friday, 9 December, confirmed having been welcomed by Committee activists equipped with trucks for the transport of material.

Finally:

Given that Western aid could not take account of actual needs, that our country could not respond quickly enough or in sufficient quantity, and that the monies collected for reconstruction had often been used in ways that took no account of the reasons why they had been collected, we asked composer Charles Aznavour and California Governor George Deukmejian to organize, respectively, a European and an American center for the collection of funds for the benefit of the earthquake victims.

We can see that the structure put into place by the Committee in the preceding months to assist refugees proved useful in the initial relief efforts. Beyond the Committee, the people of

Yerevan exhibited great solidarity during these days. A witness who did "on the spot" surveys recalls that:

> In Yerevan there was an admirable mutual aid response. For example, city residents who went to give their blood would reenter the line to give a second time. They immediately offered their medicines, their clothes, their food. Many left for Leninakan in their cars which caused gigantic traffic jams.

The First Relief Efforts

Lacking an intervention plan similar to the French ORSEC plan and an emergency structure similar to SAMU, the first assistance was given by the victims in their own immediate environment. "The people worked with whatever they had around them," sums up one witness. What was inevitably insufficient from the start often revealed itself to be fatal.

The director of a factory in Spitak told a witness about his participation in the first relief efforts:

> I was in a car on the road to Spitak when the ground trembled. I didn't quite understand what was happening. When I arrived in Spitak, I discovered the horror. The city had collapsed, as though in a bombing raid. I took a truck and went to Yerevan seeking help. With sixty young men, I returned in the early afternoon. But we lacked everything we needed to be effective. We didn't have a saw, a crane. . . . We did succeed in freeing ten students from the ruins of a school. But it took four hours to free an adolescent girl pinned against a wall, her leg crushed by the concrete. Without saying a word, she never took her eyes off her best friend. Finally, when we were able to free her, the girl threw herself into the arms of her best friend. She held him tight for an hour, without wanting to move.

During these first relief efforts, the soldiers in the Leninakan barracks were nowhere to be seen.

This same witness tells us about a physician from Yerevan who retraces his steps:

> We heard of the disaster on 7 December at about two in the afternoon. After gathering whatever we could find that might be useful, we left at three o'clock. When we arrived, it was a nightmare come true. Wounded and dead everywhere. People pulled me in every direction. "Come save my brother, come save my father." What could I do with my thirty disposable syringes? With the same syringe I innoculated ten people. Very quickly, I was all out.

An Armen-Press photographer who arrived at the site less than two hours after the catastrophe confided to another witness:

> The scale of the destruction drove people crazy and each person focused on his own family. Those who were at the factory or the office ran home. They were walking over bodies.

> At one point a young man of 25 caught me by the pants. He was on the ground under a piece of concrete that was crushing him. "I cannot move it myself, I have to get help," I told him. After searching for two hours, I was able to round up six young men. We removed the conrete. Sadly, the young man died from his injuries a few hours later. I also saw a man give moral support to a little girl buried under debris by talking to her through the rubble for two days. Finally, on 9 December the rescue workers got her out. The girl held on to him for four hours, refusing all care.

A third witness confided:

> One evening we were invited to eat at an Armenian home and a man said to me, "My uncle was trapped

under the rocks, his leg was crushed and we couldn't pull him out of there. He said to me, 'The best thing you can do for me is to get a hatchet and cut my leg off; at least it will get me out of here; otherwise I am going to lose all of my blood.'" The man showed me a hatchet and added, "With this hatchet I cut off my uncle's leg. He is still living several days later."

A witness who is a surgeon related:

> All those who participated in the first relief efforts were broken by the fact that there was practically nothing they could do. Some doctors went back home to Yerevan the same night. I won't allow myself to judge them.

On Friday, 9 December, during the day, the first relief workers from outside of Yerevan arrived; they were made up of Georgians from Akhalkalak, an area with a large number of Armenians. The schools were the first priority for these workers, and they saved several children.

This same day, in the evening, 800 young people arrived from Mountainous Karabagh. They had trucks, cranes, bulldozers, pneumatic picks, and bolt cutters to break up the reinforcing rods. The team included three doctors, including one anesthesiologist, and they brought food with them for a month.

The first units of the French detachment arrived in Leninakan on Friday, 9 December, at 9:15 p.m., bringing to a close the first relief phase. The French took the place of numerous worn-out Armenian volunteers who returned to Yerevan that evening.

Let us now examine why the earthquake claimed so many victims.

A MAJOR CATASTROPHE

In disaster medicine, an occurrence with over 1,000 deaths and over 250 people hospitalized with serious injuries is called a major catastrophe. Even before trying to estimate the number of victims more accurately, it is clear from the evidence that this was a major catastrophe. On 17 December 1988 the Soviet authorities admitted having identified 23,900 people who died because of the earthquake.[5]

Moreover, the official Soviet statistics (which were confirmed by a witness) estimated more than 15,000 injured. That makes this earthquake the most deadly in the world during the past ten years.[6]

The very heavy losses of the 7 December 1988 earthquake were not a result of the force of the two tremors. Insufficient attention to possible disasters during the planning and construction of many buildings, as well as to the organization and quality of medical help, are the source of the tragic consequences.

It was well known that the geodynamics of the affected zone made an earthquake probable in due course but the exact time and place could not be specified. This has been known by geologists for twenty years. The fault at the heart of the 7 December 1988 earthquake appears clearly on a geological map dated 1971. Like many other faults in the region, it resulted from pressure between the Arabian plate and the Russian continental plate.

In the months preceding December 1988 three different reliable sources established physical parameters that indicated a 55 percent chance of an earthquake in the near future. Finally, a Communist official in Leninakan, who would have little need to fabricate a rumor of this sort, confided to a witness that:

> In the days immediately preceding the earthquake, there was an advance signal that could have alerted the authorities: the sudden disappearance of animals, notably birds, in particular north of Leninakan.

Whatever the predictability of an earthquake in the months and days preceding 7 December may have been, its likelihood in due time was indisputable.

What happened on 7 December 1988? The Arabian and Russian continental plates overlapped, and the resulting pressure exceeded the resistance of the earth's crust, causing it to rupture.[7] The rupture was 20 to 25 kilometers long and visible along the surface for 8 kilometers. It began south of Spitak and ran toward the west northwest. The thrust reached a maximum of 1.5 meters vertically and 0.4 meters horizontally. The epicenter was between 10 and 15 kilometers wide. The earthquake consisted of two tremors at 11:41 a.m. and 11:45 a.m., with a force of 6.9 and 5.8.

If people lack the ability to prevent earthquakes, they can at least, when the likelihood is present, actively anticipate a disaster by taking three measures to limit the consequences: (1) ensure quality construction and (2–3) invest in a well-organized and quality healthcare delivery system. In the final analysis, these measures result from a culture that accords priority to the individual.

Without going into recent developments in earthquake construction, we note that quality masonry can often resist a shock of 6.9. As for the science of earthquake construction, it seeks out those structural elements of buildings which can resist the hazardous movement produced by shock waves. The preventative measures add only 2 percent to construction costs, according to V. E. Davidovici, president of the French Association of Seismic Engineering.

Quality medical relief must be well organized and effectively delivered. The organization cannot be set up on short notice; in emergency situations it must swing into action with autonomous actors, well-practiced logistics, and very rapid communications. Quality medical relief is directed at limiting the number of deaths among the survivors. It is a direct function of the level of medical development in the affected country.

The size and scope of the 7 December 1988 catastrophe is a result of two basic factors. The principal cause—and by far the more deadly—was the inability of numerous buildings to safeguard their inhabitants by absorbing the seismic shocks and even allowing for areas of survival, i.e., free space among the ruins. The second cause was the inadequate organization and quality of the first medical relief efforts.

Many buildings could not resist the earthquake while others managed to safeguard their occupants. Buildings that did not collapse were constructed during the period before and after 1950. All of them possessed one or more safety features: a simple form likely to resist seismic shocks, masonry constructed according to the standards of the trade and well maintained, and structural elements that were properly connected.

A house built close to the ground well before the development of anti-seismic construction techniques, with masonry correctly applied, and built near the earthquake fault, withstood the shock. The same was true for prefabricated buildings of 9 to 16 stories built after 1950 using a technique of assembling sections of large panels with serrated edges and interlocking metal hoops tied together with steel to form a lock. These held up quite well, safeguarding their residents. This proves that prefabricated construction, when well thought out and properly constructed, is suitable for living in seismic zones.

Finally, certain public works and buildings exhibited good earthquake resistance, proving that seismic-resistant construction is possible in the Soviet Union. Bridges, tunnels, electrical transformers, and the like suffered little or no damage.

Hospitals, on the other hand—public buildings that are urgently needed during a disaster—collapsed for the most part, taking with them two-thirds of the doctors, medical infrastructure, materials, and medicines.

These four factors together reduced the possibility of an effective medical response during the first stage of relief.

The hospitals, like all of the collapsed buildings, had one or more of the following problems:

1. The collapsed buildings did not take advantage of state-of-the-art international knowledge concering the design and execution of links between structural elements. This failure is the result of the isolation of Soviet society, which restricts access to the latest international scientifc developments, a problem also found in numerous other countries.

Experts in seismic engineering dispatched to the disaster areas pointed out the inadequacy of linkages between structural elements. "The majority of partial or total collapses is a result of faulty mechanical links between structural elements and/or the fact that the linkages were more rigid than flexible," states the preliminary technical report of the French Association of Seismic Engineering's mission in Armenia.

The drawback of brittle linkages is that they can snap in an earthquake, whereas flexible linkages absorb part of the shock without precipitating a collapse. The report concludes that a large number of collapsed floor panels were assembled by simply lining up prefabricated honeycombed panels and linking them at the ends without any steel reinforcement.

2. These specialists also noticed a level of workmanship that was less than desirable, both in the lack of care in linking structural elements and in the quality of the materials used. Poor cement quality was not the primary cause of the destruction, contrary to what was said by numerous non-expert witnesses. Cement of excellent quality is not sufficient by itself to prevent panels from collapsing on top of each other without leaving any survival pockets.

These serious defects in the design and execution of much of the construction lead us to doubt the existence of serious quality-control inspection in the Soviet Union.

Estimates of Destruction

The estimates of earthquake destruction include two dimensions. First is the period of construction. One-seventh of the buildings destroyed were built before 1950.

Three factors play an important role here: insufficient horizontal and vertical masonry linkages, the use of complicated forms with little earthquake resistance,[8] and insufficient maintenance. The rest, constructed after this date, consist notably of numerous prefabricated nine-story buildings in Leninakan, with insufficient linkages between posts and beams. The majority of industrial buildings collapsed for the same reasons.

The second dimension is the percentage of destruction as a function of location. The city of Spitak and the village of Nalband, both close to the epicenter, were practically 100 percent destroyed. The city of Leninakan was 75 percent destroyed. The cities of Kirovakan and Stepanavan were seriously damaged. Added to this are about fifty villages, many of which were seriously affected. Of these, Saraart and Gogaran are close to Spitak.

The major scope of this catastrophe can be attributed first of all to the inappropriate construction of many buildings for withstanding seismic shocks. In California, thanks to quality earthquake-resistant construction methods, an earthquake of this magnitude would cause "probably no deaths, and certainly no more than a dozen" according to V. E. Davidovici. The tragic consequences of this 7 December 1988 earthquake begin with the social organization of Armenian society.

In Soviet Armenia, because of the very small number of survival pockets in the rubble, even the best rescue system would have saved barely more than several hundred lives. In addition to the poor adaptability of many buildings, the first relief efforts suffered from poor governmental organization and poor-quality medicine. These factors further increased the human toll of the cataclysm.

Poor Governmental Organization and Insufficient Medical Resources

By its very nature, a major catastrophe always exceeds all available resources, an additional reason for advanced planning. Soviet authorities and the Soviet press recognized many times that an efficient rescue organization was badly lacking. This void left the initiative to the Karabagh Committee for two and a half days. Whatever the good intentions of the Committee, its actions inevitably suffered from a lack of preparation and from its non-official status. As an expression of popular will, the Committee had no chance to mobilize state resources, such as the Soviet army, which could have proven useful under the circumstances. The absence of competent official spokespersons did nothing to facilitate the efforts of well-intentioned people.[9]

To that we must add mediocre medical help, which contributed to the death of a large majority of the injured in the hours and days following the earthquake. In the final anaysis, this poor quality stems from the backwardness of Soviet medicine in areas of competence, equipment, and pharmacology. Witnesses from the medical relief corps estimate this lag at fifteen to forty years behind French medicine.

Without going into details, this results in the notorious incompetence of 70 to 90 percent of Soviet physicians, especially in resuscitation technology and care for victims of crush syndrome. The ability of Soviet nurses is no greater than that of French nurses aides. The level of sanitation is unsatisfactory, especially in operating rooms. With regard to materials, the Soviet Minister of Health himself admits the general deficiencies: one stethoscope in two, he made known, does not work at the point of leaving the factory.[10]

Before the earthquake, in theory, Yerevan had eleven dialysis centers dating from the 1960s. In fact, seven of them no longer worked. In the days following the catastrophe, two of the four remaining machines broke down. This machinery was cruelly lacking for the victims of crush syndrome. Finally, pharmaceuticals suffered from qualitative and quantitative shortcomings, especially antibiotics, which are essential for the care of all sorts of wounds and traumas.

It is estimated that at least 15,000 people were injured and some physicians tried their best to assist them. Two-thirds of these were injured in the collapse of buildings at the moment of the earthquake when they were in the streets. One-third were buried near the surface of the rubble and were freed as quickly as possible. They were not removed or revived with any great skill. They were taken to Yerevan in poorly suited vehicles and 10,000 died before reaching the capital.

Of the 5,000 injured who survived the journey, at least 3,000 died within three days of the earthquake, bringing to 13,000 the number of injured who died. This represents a mortality rate of 87 percent. Less than 2,000 injured people survived the first week after the earthquake, for a survival rate of 13 percent.

This very high mortality rate can be attributed to the initial rescue efforts. Whatever the good intentions of the people may have been, without proper training or medical knowledge, they could not free, care for, and transport a seriously injured person. Victims of concussion, chest and abdominal traumas, and internal bleeding present demanding treatment problems. Only highly competent and perfectly trained and equipped medical teams such as SAMU can make any claim to success. In the absence of such teams, these seriously injured people will practically all die during the acute phase of an emergency.

As for the Soviet physicians—underequipped, without hospitals, ignorant of the principles of emergency medical triage—how could they be expected to have anything but a limited impact? Furthermore, crush syndrome—the trauma associated with collapses or cave-ins—was unknown to Soviet doctors.

From a description of crush syndrome given by a French doctor, the physician-director of a Leninakan hospital recognized that he had seen 100 people a day suffering from it during the first three days, for a minimum of 300 victims in this one area alone. This syndrome, which requires precise and rapid treatment to prevent sudden death or kidney failure, was not treated properly. The absence of proper care, medications, and dialysis led to the deaths of nearly all the victims of crush syndrome during the week following the earthquake, before the arrival of the first dialysis machines from abroad.

As a result of this general situation, about 2,000 people with comparatively light injuries—generally with fractures of limbs—were the only ones to survive the first rescue efforts. Too often, therapeutic errors and poor sanitary conditions after the delivery of first aid led to gangrene. Surgeons had to carry out amputations that could have been avoided.

The Human Toll

The majority of witnesses—veterans of numerous disasters and thus able to provide reliable estimates—agreed on a figure of 100,000 for the minimum number of deaths from the earthquake. Three others put the figure at between 100,000 and 150,000.

This minimum figure of 100,000 deaths seems all the more plausible when we consider that a coordinator for Doctors without Borders, not of Armenian background and well-informed, fixed the number of deaths in Leninakan (population 300,000) at 70,000. If we add to this the victims of the city of Spitak (population 27,000), which was nearly 100 percent destroyed; Kirovakan (population 170,000); Stepanavan (population 40,000); the large number of victims among the 100,000 Armenians from Azerbaijan who had sought refuge in the region after fleeing the pogroms during the preceding several months; and the casualties in the 50 or so villages affected, including Nalband where 1,800 of 2,000 inhabitants perished; the figure of 100,000 seems to be a bottom-line estimate.

Given that the Armenian population living in Soviet Armenia is 3,300,000 people, these deaths represented 3.03 percent of the population.

Extrapolating this onto the population of France,[11] this figure would represent 1,692,558 deaths. This exceeds the number of French deaths from combat, combat wounds, illnesses contracted during military service, POW captivity, and missing-in-action status during World War I.[12] This extrapolated figure would practically wipe out the population of Marseilles, estimated in 1986 at 1,753,000 people. These comparative figures put the scope of the national disaster of 7 December 1988 into perspective.

The Soviet figures require some discussion. The Soviet Chief of State Nicholai Ryjkov arrived in Armenia on Thursday, 8 December 1988, and estimated the number of dead and missing at 100,000, a figure announced on the front page of *Le Monde* placed on sale on Friday, 9 December and dated the 10th.

On Saturday morning, 10 December, the first official tally tentatively stated "at least 45,000 dead and 12,000 injured." [13] Tuesday, 13 December, a new official tally stated 50,000 fatalities.[14] Monday, 19 December, *Le Monde* put the issue dated the 20th on sale, citing information from Tass dated the 17th. It declared that 23,390 victims had been identified and declared dead from the earthquake. The same Soviet source estimated that an equal number remained buried in the rubble.

However, on Thursday, 29 December, a mid-level political functionary upset everyone. He declared that only 25,000 people had perished. He added that he expected only 100 to 200 more bodies to be removed from the rubble.[15]

We could ask ourselves about the reasons for this announcement, which completely contradicted the official tally of 13 December. The important thing is to notice that this is an amalgam of the approximate number of bodies extracted from the ruins and identified by that date and the total number of victims. The announcement of the 29th also contradicts the dispatch of the 17th on the matter of bodies still buried in the rubble.

The statement on 29 December in no way overrides the witnesses' estimates of 100,000 dead as a bottom-line estimate. The clash between this latter figure and that of 23,390 removed from the ruins by 17 December leads us to conclude that three-fourths of the earthquake victims remained "missing," with the search efforts slowing down after that date.

Finally, this earthquake left a large number of people homeless due to the destruction or damage of so many buildings. On this matter, the witnesses are in agreement with Soviet authorities: between 500,000 and 700,000 people, or about 60 percent of the population living in the earthquake areas, were left without shelter.

NOTES

1. Contrary to the genocide, which the Armenians feel is not always recognized by the international community, this second catastrophe is already a part of world history, in a certain sense, because of the role played by the mass media.

2. Referring to this strategy, *Le Monde*, dated 6 December 1988, announced "The Kremlin Wants to Retake Control of Law and Order in the Caucasus."

3. *Le Monde*, 2 December 1988.

4. *Quotidien de Paris*, 16 December 1988, article by Francois Raoux.

5. Figure cited by Tass and published by *Le Monde*, 20 December 1988.

6. According to the *Quotidien de Paris*, dated 9 December 1988, the earthquake of 16 September 1973 in eastern Iran left 25,000 dead, the Mexican earthquake of 19 September 1985, 5,000 dead, and El Asnam, Algeria, 10 October 1980, 2,590 dead. The deadliest earthquake of the twentieth century struck on 26 July 1976 and destroyed the city of Tangshan, near Peking. The official tally registered 242,000 victims, but experts put the number at 700,000. One French expert says these figures underestimate the realities, in particular for the Mexican earthquake.

7. For a detailed description of the movement of continental masses see Yvonne Rebeyral, "Between the Jaws of a Vice," *Le Monde*, 11 December 1988.

8. A fundamental principle of seismic engineering is that simple forms, the cylinder and the square and even the rectangle, resist earthquake forces better than

non-simple forms. On this subject see V. E. Davidovici, "Seismic Design Begins with the Choice of Building Shapes," # 97, *Cahiers du Bâtiment* (March 1988).

9. According to A. Manoutcharian in his text already cited in this chapter.

10. Cited in the June 1989 issue of *Géopolitique* devoted to the U.S.S.R. under Gorbachev.

11. Estimated in 1988 at 55,860,000 inhabitants, "World Statistics, 1989," *Universal Encyclopedia*.

12. 1,400,000 people according to R. Remond, *Notre Siècle* [Our Century] (Fayard, 1988), p. 22.

13. *Le Monde*, 11 December 1988.

14. *Quotidien de Paris*, 16 December 1988; *Le Monde*, 20 December 1988.

15. *Le Monde*, 31 December 1988.

CHAPTER 2

Foreign Relief Aid Arrives

Was it possible for foreign relief assistance to arrive earlier at the disaster sites and lower, even if ever so slightly, the number of victims? In order to answer this question, we must examine the step-by-step organization of the relief efforts. We are particularly interested in aid organized by the French–Armenian diasporan community, the French government, and private organizations working on site such as Doctors without Borders.

The Soviet government's authorization for foreign organizations to bring their relief efforts to the disaster victims produced an international solidarity movement with few parallels. Several dozen nations participated in this mobilization to aid the victims. On 17 December, the Soviet ambassador to France spoke of "seventy-seven nations" that had participated in emergency relief efforts.

This vast collective effort was based in the idea that no effort should be spared to save even a single life. The widespread media attention given to the disaster also contributed to promoting consciousness of the events; in turn, this promoted the growth of sympathy. Other humanitarian causes have also been publicized by the press, and they have often reached a larger number of persons, but they have not aroused a comparable level of solidarity.

In this international mobilization, the identity of the victims seems important and is linked to several different motivations. "On the one hand," reflects an Armenian in the diaspora:

> everybody knows the Armenians. They have been a part of history since Biblical times. On the other hand, the 1915 Armenian genocide weighs heavily on the conscience of the world. Finally, the diaspora, which stems from the genocide, is generally well integrated and does not arouse antipathy. Quite the contrary.[1]

Another diasporan Armenian wonders if:

> This reaction originates in the unconscious desire of the international community to redeem itself for abandoning the Armenians at the time of the genocide and later over the issue of the recognition of the genocide.

A non-Armenian witness thinks that:

> The identification of Westerners with the victims takes place easily in the case of the Armenians because they are seen as being a part of European culture.

Finally, the outpouring of Armenian political activism during the months preceding the catastrophe helped many people to remember them.

Before examining the mobilization of governmental and private aid in France, let us consider the activities of the diaspora.

SOLIDARITY IN THE FRENCH–ARMENIAN DIASPORA

As early as Thursday, 8 December 1988 at 9 a.m., an emergency medical team composed of three surgeons, a physician, and an anesthesiologist—Armenians or Armenophiles—was equipped and ready to proceed to the disaster sites. This team waited until noon on Saturday, 10 December 1988, for authorization from the Soviet authorities to travel to the disaster zones.

One of the team members observed:

> Precious hours were lost because it is during the first
> thirty-six hours that physicians can save the most lives.
> In contrast to the journalists, for whom the level of crisis
> is different, the physicians deeply regret this delay in
> opening the borders.

Doctors without Borders was in contact with one of the Armenian surgeons as early as Wednesday afternoon, and these volunteers were integrated into the first DWB flight. This flight took off from Brussels on Saturday, 10 December, at 9 p.m.; after a stop in Moscow, it touched down in Yerevan on Sunday, 11 December, at 7 a.m. In addition to these five physicians, fifty or so additional Armenian diasporan physicians presented their credentials as early as Thursday morning.

Besides the dimension of medical solidarity, we must add the activities of the entire diasporan community. These activities resulted from the trauma created by the disaster in their homeland.

The Resurgence of Armenian Ethnic Identity in the Diaspora

Prior to the disaster, the Armenian diasporan community in France saw its identity threatened by two factors: assimilation and division. A diasporan Armenian of about 30 years of age explains:

> If the Christian faith of the Armenians reinforces their
> identity in Moslem countries, in predominantly Catholic
> countries like France, this faith works insidiously to pro-
> mote assimilation since it represents a common cultural
> tradition.

> In addition, we wake up every day in an environment
> where everything is written in French, where the cus-
> toms and values are obviously not those of our forefa-
> thers, so how can we preserve an Armenian identity?
> Confronted with this dilemma, members of the diaspora
> choose one of the three following options:

Some wish to forget their identity and cut themselves off from Armenian history, which has too often been marked by ill fate. Others, on the contrary, carefully cultivate their identity and pass it on from generation to generation. Finally, the majority suffers from a duality and is pulled between the two tendencies above.

On the eve of the earthquake, Armenian identity in the diaspora was relatively quiet.

Division also threatened identity. The major line of cleavage in the community concerned relations with Soviet Armenia, and beyond that with the Soviet state itself. Communists, bourgeois liberals, and ASALA* advocated unconditional support for Soviet Armenia, while the Armenian Revolutionary Federation (*Dashnaksoutioun*),+ inspired by socialism, defended the idea of a "Free, Independent, and United Armenia." Other differences added themselves to this one, and the result was that the Armenian diaspora could agree on an idea and a course of collective action only with great difficulty.

The earthquake of 7 December 1988 changed this situation in a single stroke by reviving Armenian identity in the heart of the diaspora and creating solidarity around the issue of aid to the earthquake victims. It is clear to Armenians and non-Armenians that the earthquake strengthened Armenian identity in the diaspora as no other event could have. In effect, whatever

---

* *Translator's note:* Armenian Secret Army for the Liberation of Armenia (ASALA) was a left-wing Armenian paramilitary organization based in the Middle East in the late 1970s and early 1980s. It was responsible for the assassinations of numerous Turkish diplomats worldwide. ASALA's ultimate, yet unfulfilled, objective was joint revolutionary struggle in Turkey by Kurdish, Turkish, and Armenian forces.

+ *Translator's note:* The Armenian Revolutionary Federation (ARF) is a major Armenian political party founded in Tbilisi, Georgia, in 1890. The party headed the government of independent Armenia in 1918–1920. Although socialism played an important part in party ideology in its early years, the ARF after 1920 became an outspoken nationalist critic of Soviet Armenia. After the fall of the Soviet Union, the ARF functioned as a legal opposition party in the new Republic of Armenia. This changed in early 1995 when the Ter Petrossian government had the ARF—including its party press, youth organizations, etc.—banned for six months. Charges leveled at the ARF included narcotics and weapons trafficking and terrorism, including political assassination. All charges have been denied by the ARF leadership.

may have been their prior relationship to the homeland as a part of their total identity as persons, all members of the diaspora were deeply distressed by the disaster.

A diasporan Armenian, aged thirty, whose identification with the community had been weak, summarized this process when he said, "December 7th echoed in me." The day after the catastrophe, Robert Belleret of *Le Monde* described the Armenian Cultural Center in Lyons:

> Everyone looks very anxious and the sadness bears down. An immense map of Armenia takes up an entire wall and serves to limit the obliterated areas in people's hearts and minds. A bearded worker of about 40 who had left Armenia eight years ago is consumed by worry. Two of his cousins live near the epicenter.[2]

Everyone whose national identity had been weakened by the diasporan experience found it reasserting itself when confronted with this collective tragedy. Several Armenian witnesses from the diaspora confided that their participation in the relief effort in Armenia allowed them to reclaim their identity. For example, one third-generation diasporan Armenian said:

> Until now I have never suffered as an Armenian. Now because of our tragic past, it is difficult to tell yourself that you are an Armenian if you haven't suffered.

By contrast, another diasporan Armenian said he refused to let himself be trapped in the circle of tragedy, which to him seemed to define Armenian history. He saw his participation in the relief project as a way of leaving this circle of pain "by abandoning the role of the victim for the role of the helper."

Whatever may have been the complexity of their motivations, all diasporan Armenians felt a powerful need to contribute to the assistance of disaster victims.

We find these feelings and this solidarity rooted fundamentally in a collective Armenian concern with their actual physical survival as a minority. Haunted by the genocide, they naturally overcame their differences when it became a question of national survival. The power of this force was such that those who had the ability to go to Armenia to participate directly in the relief efforts sensed a feeling of jealousy on the part of those who, for one reason or another, had to remain behind in the diaspora to collect donations.

The outcome of this painful revival of identity was the coming together of a large majority of the diasporan community to organize relief efforts during the night of 7 December and the day of the 8th. Two organizations united their efforts: SOS/Armenia,[3] which was created for this emergency around the three Armenian churches (Apostolic, Catholic, and Protestant), and the Armenian Blue Cross of France, a preexisting organization affiliated with the Armenian Revolutionary Federation (*Dashnaksoutioun*).

For a month the diasporan community went through an energetic revival that had no precedent. One member of the diaspora recalls that, "The Armenians were everywhere, like ants, collecting, packing, and dispatching aid." The horror of 7 December 1988 will leave its mark on the history of the diaspora for a long time.

NON-DIASPORAN FRENCH SOLIDARITY

Contrary to 1915, Armenians would not be alone during the tragedy of 1988. Many non-Armenian citizens and organizations as well as government agencies would prove their commitment. In this vast international movement, the French would distinguish themselves by the number of relief workers they sent.

French Governmental Aid

The operational center of Public Safety* learned of the disaster by means of a telex from Agence France-Presse on

* *Translator's note:* Public Safety is a function of the Ministry of the Interior. It consists of 2.5 million people, firemen, and volunteers, for the protection of people, property, and the environment in the wake of catastrophes. Public Safety works locally in cooperation with prefects (department) and mayors (city and town).

Wednesday the 7th, shortly before noon. The center began by confirming the report through the Institute of World Geography in Strasbourg, the Soviet Embassy in Paris, and the French Embassy in Moscow. At the same time, in order not to lose time, the center conducted an inventory of available relief materials. An earthquake of this magnitude in an inhabited area was verified in the afternoon. The inventory of material and human resources and planes was completed during the night.

As usual, and although several higher-level persons at Public Safety doubted that the Soviet state would authorize intervention by a foreign government, standard operating procedures were followed; the airborne disaster emergency units (DICA) were put on alert on the night of the 7th. These were instructional and intervention units of Public Safety (USIIC), # 1, based at Nogent-le-Rotrou, and # 7, based at Brignoles. Each DICA unit was made up of 60 men, 6 dogs, and 6 tons of cargo. Everything can be mobilized in three hours; the unit is self-sufficient for a week, and can be divided into three operational groups. These two DICA units were ready for takeoff during the early hours of 8 December.

On the morning of the 8th, Public Safety also put on alert the medical support detachment (DAM 30), the disaster relief detachment of SAMU 94, the disaster detachment of the southeast zone, and the disaster detachment of Ile-de-France.

Once government authorization was received on the 8th at 7 p.m., the order was given for the detachments to proceed to the airports at Istres and Villacoublay. After loading, the first wave took off on the 9th at 5:40 a.m. and 6:45 a.m. in two Hercules C-130s from COTAM. These two planes carried 169 people, of which 22 were physicians, 19 cynophile teams (dogs and their masters specially trained to search for walled-in bodies buried in rubble), and one veterinarian. They represented USIIC 1, USIIC 7, SAMU 94, DAM 30, and COLMED 16. They were under the command of DACO. The planes landed in Yerevan on 9 December at 4 p.m. and 5 p.m. local time.

After unloading their cargo into trucks and taking the road from Yerevan to Leninakan, the first group from the French detachments arrived on the earthquake site on 9 December at 9:15 p.m.

The second relief wave took off on the 10th in two DC 8s from COTAM at 5:35 a.m. and 6:10 a.m. It was made up of 166 people, including 10 physicians, 36 cynophile teams, and 2 veterinarians, all from DICA, Ile-de-France, and Southeast. On the 11th at 5 p.m. and the 12th at 3 a.m., a DC 8 and a Hercules C-130 from COTAM carried 20 people in charge of logistical support along with 27 tons of cargo in the third wave. The fourth and last wave left French soil on the 12th at 10:19 p.m. on an Airbus A300 from Air France. It carried 144 people from a fire brigade in Paris and a battalion of naval fire fighters from Marseilles.

In total there were 499 people, 55 dogs, and 77.5 tons of cargo. The monetary value of governmental aid exceeded 19 million francs.[4]

Non-Governmental French Aid

Several private French organizations, including Doctors without Borders (DWB), participated in helping the victims.

How did DWB mobilize resources? The first telex announcing the earthquake alluded to 160 deaths. DWB began by verifying this information before beginning preparations. At the same time, DWB analyzed the possibilities for action.

The Soviet Union had never, up until this time, opened its borders to private organizations and many doubted the possibility of any type of a mission. In the best case, they thought, only governmental aid would be approved.

On Thursday, 8 December, the disaster toll was known to be much more serious than the initial telex indicated. DWB left its visa applications with the Soviet authorities, all the while remaining skeptical about the possibility of a positive response. At the same time, in order not to lose time in case the response was positive, DWB began gathering relief supplies. On Friday the 9th, the Soviet Embassy in Paris assured DWB that permission to intervene might be granted shortly. This led DWB to conclude that a mission was possible.[5]

From this point, everything moved very quickly. DWB set its European intervention unit into motion, regrouping its French, Belgian, Dutch, Spanish, Swiss, and Luxembourgian sections. A member of DWB France spent the day with the Soviet representative in Paris, and Friday night obtained authorization to intervene. The same day, DWB contacted physicians and logistical coordinators at the same time that they were mobilizing their materials, thanks to emergency stockpiles.

On Saturday, 10 December, members of the Armenian team (who had been ready since Thursday the 8th) obtained their visas and joined the first DWB team. Together they left for Brussels where a plane leaving for Armenia awaited them. It took off at 9 p.m. with one DWB team made up of 3 surgeons, 2 anesthesiologists, 2 physicians, and 4 logistical coordinators. In the cargo area they carried medical and surgical equipment, temporary shelters, survival blankets, electrical generators, and two Soviet four-wheel drive vehicles. These would provide the team with the precious freedom of movement they would need during the first days of the mission.

After stopping in Moscow (where they lost four hours to change flight crews), the first DWB plane landed in Armenia on 11 December 1988 at 7 a.m. While this plane was arriving, other members of the organization were making preparations to depart within a few days. DWB in France began to put together "Operation Dialysis" in order to aid the victims of "crush syndrome." [6]

The way in which this was done is interesting. From the start, DWB wanted to be able to operate independently and be able to adapt to the specific situations they would encounter. Also, the mission coordinator for Marseilles chose her equipment according to the criteria of strength and durability; she was able to put together a complete dialysis team made up of a nephrologist, a nurse capable of operating the machines, a technician well versed in installing and repairing them, a physician with a specialty in the biological sciences qualified to set up a medical analysis laboratory, and an anesthesiologist for reviving the patients. The result was that the DWB team was operational from the start, whereas many others were not.

Thirty-five hours after the start of the mission, on Monday the 12th at 9:30 p.m., a nephrologist, a specialized nurse, and a medical technician took off from Marseilles with five kidney dialysis machines and all the necessary support materials and equipment. After a stopover in Paris to join other members from DWB, they left France on Tuesday, 13 December at 10 p.m. They landed in Yerevan on Wednesday, 14 December at 10:30 p.m., delayed by weather conditions over the capital that forced a one-night stopover in Turkey.

Since the physician-biologist and anesthesiologist took off the same Wednesday from Marseilles and arrived without delay, the equipment was ready to use. The technician had installed at least one of the machines by Thursday the 15th at noon, and the mission was operational. Two persons were under dialysis by Friday, 16 December.

In total the teams from DWB would care for fifteen victims of crush syndrome. Unfortunately, the call for international aid came too late—four days after the earthquake—and nearly all of the victims of crush syndrome had already died. The basic cause of this delay was the inability of Soviet physicians to diagnose crush syndrome properly and to provide the appropriate care. The lack of competent nephrologists in Armenia delayed the appeal for international aid until the arrival of foreign doctors; this caused four precious days to be lost.

Now let us consider the question posed at the start of the chapter: Could aid from France have reached the disaster sites earlier than it did? A chronological study of aid mobilization leads us to answer in the positive. If the Soviets had authorized access to the disaster sites immediately, the French units would have been there less than thirty-six hours after the disaster, and assistance from the diasporan community would have arrived by Friday night—indeed, even by Thursday night. Care of the injured and help for those trapped under rubble would have been greatly ameliorated.

This having been said, it remains difficult to estimate precisely the number of lives that might have been saved, and we should not lose sight of the fact that the major cause of this catastrophe was poor construction methods rather than the relief efforts.

Doctors without Borders could have arrived in the earthquake zone anywhere from twelve to twenty-four hours earlier. The fact that "Operation Dialysis" was organized in thirty-five hours by DWB demonstrates that it would have been possible to save a larger number of crush syndrome victims if the appeal for international aid had been made sooner by the Soviet physicians. To counterbalance this observation, we must note that the humanitarian organizations had insufficient experience in earthquake intervention and were late in including dialysis equipment in their initial response to the disaster.

NOTES

1. Over half of the 6 to 7 million Armenians worldwide live outside of the borders of Soviet Armenia, one of the 15 republics of the U.S.S.R. This present dispersal stems directly from the 1915 genocide. Those who escaped sought refuge in Transcaucasia, Syria, Lebanon, and Greece. They remained there or migrated westward in the wake of economic and political crises. In Turkey, there are now no more than 70,000 Armenians. Without freedom of association, the diaspora within the Soviet Union, which numbers 1.5 million people, lacks a community structure. The rest of the diaspora is scattered among the five continents with large concentrations in the Middle East, France (250,000 to 300,000 people), the United States, Argentina, and Brazil.

2. *Le Monde*, 11 December 1988.

3. Under the title "SOS/Armenia: An Emergency Structure Created During the First Hours that Followed the Tragedy" the monthly *France Arménie* featured this organization in its January 1989 issue:

> At the request of the three church communities, the Armenian Apostolic Church, the Catholic Church, and the Evangelical Church, an emergency action organization was created on 8 December 1988 with its headquarters at 15 rue de la Jean-Goujon, Paris VIII.

> SOS/Armenia was conceived of as a single unit with four areas of specialization: social, financial, material, and media. While operating independently, SOS/Armenia nevertheless has the support of other French organizations and works with the Blue Cross of Armenians of France and is in regular communication with Doctors without Borders and Physicians International.

> In the short term, SOS/Armenia is responding to the urgent needs imposed by the earthquake; alerting the international community, organizing relief collections, and ensuring the delivery of these donations.

4. See the "emergency section" government report.

5. The first plane carrying Doctors without Borders members took off on Saturday, 10 December in the morning and arrived during the night of Saturday/Sunday after a stopover in Istanbul.

6. Dialysis compensates for kidney deficiencies by clearing toxic matter that spreads through the body after the crushed victim has been freed from the rubble.

PART II

A
TRAUMATIZED
POPULATION

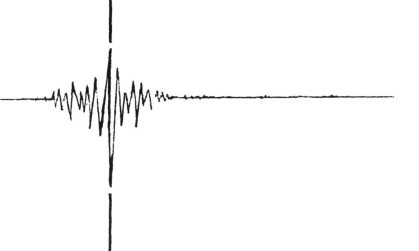

CHAPTER 3

The Foreign Relief Workers

This chapter is dedicated to trapped survivors who were saved by foreign relief workers, especially the French. However, the chapter opens with a tribute to Soviet citizens, both Armenians and others.

One witness recounts:

> One week after the earthquake, an Armenian, like many others, continued to dig with only his hands and a pick axe for tools. His fingertips were badly torn up and bloodied. A doctor told him, "If you continue to dig, we will have to amputate." He answered, "What do my hands matter, everything I cherish is under there—my son, my daughter, my wife, my mother."

Two other witnesses reported that Soviet civilians, often young non-Armenians, "also worked like crazy, without sleeping or eating."

On 17 December 1988, when most of the foreign relief workers had left on the orders of the Soviet government, these local workers continued their search, often wearing gas masks to protect themselves from the stench of bodies in the ruins.

As for the Soviet army, it did not participate in the search for

trapped survivors. Charged with dispatching the cranes necessary to lift the heaviest sections of collapsed buildings, the army
moved too slowly on this task to be of any real use. During the
period from 9 to 16 December, while large numbers of foreign
relief workers were there, the needed construction cranes were
lacking. They did not arrive in large numbers until 17 December. As a result, they could only be used to level the ruins that
contained no one but the dead.

On the other hand, the army vigorously enforced a tough
law-and-order code in the disaster zones as well as in Yerevan by
holding the Armenians to a strict curfew.

Despite their skill and dedication, the foreign relief
workers were not able to free more than 40 survivors, 15 of
whom owe their lives to French relief workers.

THE EFFORTS OF THE FRENCH RELIEF WORKERS

The first French relief units went to work after their
arrival in Leninakan on Friday, 9 December 1988, at 9:15 p.m.

One of the workers describes the following scene:

We found a chaotic situation, a population left to themselves. One part of the detachment went to a housing
development on the outskirts of the city. This area contained a large number of apartment buildings of nine to
twelve stories built a dozen years ago: they collapsed like
a house of cards, claiming an enormous number of victims. Around us, several families searched in the ruins of
their building, sometimes with a crane or a bulldozer.

The detachment found several survivors in this area. . . .
I remember, for example, two women. The first, pinned
between two slabs of concrete under a dozen meters of
debris, called for her father. We could make her out at
the end of a crevice. It was nightmarish. We succeeded
in reaching her and she was immediately turned over to

the medical team. We also freed another woman. She was covered up by tons of rock. I saw only one finger. We talked and I learned that she was seven months pregnant. She was denying the disaster, asking her husband if he was "busy taking care of the little one's things." We freed her, but the child was dead.

The rescue missions began with the choice of a site. The relief workers then designated their smallest geographic work units according to the possibilities laid out by the DICA technical group. To locate the most promising areas, they first had to collect information from survivors concerning the possibility of additional survivors.

The dogs, expertly trained, then proceeded through the ruins with their masters. Each pair worked as a team, since only the master is able to interpret the animal's signals. To work most effectively, the dog had to be calm and able to rest between search periods. When a dog signaled the possibility of a survivor by barking and crouching, his master rewarded him and led him away while new dogs were brought in to confirm a possible find. For further verification, a listening team used a triangular approach method to pinpoint the location of the walled-in survivor more precisely. In the case of a confirmation, the workers, now aided by Armenians, would clean and "thin out" the ruins from the top down, taking the greatest possible care not to disturb this concrete house of cards.

A large number of cranes would have been necessary to remove the heaviest slabs of concrete as quickly as possible. Specially trained relief workers took over the last few meters containing the lighter rubble. They also took charge of the survivors as soon as possible, giving them liquids by means of a pipe lowered into the rubble. After removal, the survivors were fed arterially (perfused) to combat dehydration and blood loss. If necessary, care was provided to prevent the onset of crush syndrome.

With the utmost care, the injured were moved out of the ruins and sent to an advanced medical post where the physicians prepared them for evacuation to a hospital. In total, removal of a survivor from the ruins could take twenty-four to thirty-six hours and as much as forty-five hours.

Monday, 12 December, six days after the catastrophe, French relief workers spent a day with a 36-year-old woman under the ruins of a nine-story apartment building. She had grabbed her small daughter at the moment of the earthquake, and for four days, this mother lived with the agony of her child, unable to care for her or even remove her body after she died.

Tuesday, 13 December, seven days after the earthquake, a woman named Lucie is removed from the ruins. Frédéric Bourgade, special correspondent for *Liberation* describes this event:

> Lucie, aged thirty, is trapped in a niche one meter square, under a stone stairway that managed to support the debris from a nine-story apartment house. Without food or water, they found her prostrate, suffering from hypothermia. The relief workers caught a glimpse of her from floodlights mounted on cranes, and it took seven hours to get her out. Each movement was carefully calculated. Any false move could cause a new collapse. To maintain contact, which they lost several times, the workers would speak to her, trying to reassure her. They were able to get water to her and then to hold her hand. Little by little they enlarged the hole. She freed her arm. But in the end, they had to go in and get her. "I cannot get out. I will not get out!" she cried.[1]

A rescue worker finally was able to pull her out. A physician administered Valium immediately. Unlike most of the walled-in victims, this woman had managed to maintain a sense of time.

To our knowledge, the last survivor was freed at midday on Friday, 16 December, ten days after the catastrophe. Since 7 December the father-in-law had insisted that he heard her. The old man was so persistent that the relief workers agreed to help him, and they finally got her out. She was placed in a Soviet ambulance and taken to the Second Dispensary of Doctors without Borders in Leninakan.

One of the logistical coordinators immediately started up one of the generators to provide electricity to light up the operating room. Unconscious, covered with dirt and concrete dust, the woman appeared to be about fifty years old. While cleaning her off, the doctor took an account of her condition, observing the absence of visible wounds and signs of concussion but noting several hematomas. Seriously dehydrated, her systolic blood pressure was 80 and her temperature, taken rectally, was 34° Celsius (93° Farenheit), the lowest figure available on the thermometer. Doctors without Borders slowly warmed her body and examined and perfused her.

After some time she regained consciousness and asked for news about her children and husband. She was able to tell the doctors her name and age: Anahide, 26 years old. Her temperature rose to 35 (95° F) and her pressure to 100, and the medical team planned for her evacuation in a Soviet ambulance. The team submitted a medical report to the Soviet physician who accompanied the patient to the hospital in Erubuni (Yerevan) where a French nephrologist would take charge of her care.

Doctors without Borders supplied the accompanying physician with the saline solution she would need during transport and prepared a padded stretcher for her to ensure the best possible conditions for the trip. After having placed Anahide in the hands of the French nephrologist, the Soviet physician returned the padded stretcher to the dispensary in Leninakan. From then on it was named "Anahide." [2]

Several Points to Remember Concerning the Presence of Foreign Relief Workers

Intervention by foreign relief workers began on Friday, 9 December 1988, and ended on Friday the 16th. This period may be divided into two stages. During the first, the 9th through the 13th, the foreign relief workers were at maximum strength. On the 14th, the Soviet government ordered the French to leave Spitak. On this date, foreign activity began to wind down until it ended completely on 16 December.

On Thursday the 15th, 152 French relief workers and 27 dogs left Armenia. They were followed by a second wave on the 16th and a last one on the 17th. On Friday the 16th the Soviets urged the foreign relief workers to halt further searches. These last workers left soon after.

For the survivors, the departure of the foreign relief workers ended any remaining hope that their loved ones would be found alive and marked the beginning of mourning by the surviving victims of the earthquake.

Why did the Soviet government order the withdrawal of foreign relief workers as early as 14 December when a survivor had been found on the 16th? Contrary to a rumor spread on 15 December by another private relief organization (and immediately refuted by Doctors without Borders), there was no risk of an epidemic to justify this evacuation.

The desire to level the ruins also does not seem to be the cause, since bulldozer activity remained sporadic during the following weeks. In April of 1989, the task of clearing the wreckage was far from complete.

It is always difficult to determine the end of the period of maximum effectiveness in relief efforts. It generally falls between ten and twelve days after the beginning of intervention. One of the relief workers from the group describes this withdrawal as a "political decision." Several things indicate that the withdrawal was ordered out of a desire to evacuate the surviving population—a frequent preoccupation of governments in charge of disaster areas.

From the 13th on, cars equipped with loudspeakers circulated in Leninakan ordering the population—under threat of arrest—to leave the city. According to another witness, on 15 December the Soviet authorities wanted to declare the disaster zone a no man's land to which only authorized persons would have access. The same day an armored vehicle, whose gun had been removed but equipped with a loudspeaker, again ordered the people to leave.

Around 20 December, faced with reluctant compliance, the state cut back on the distribution of natural gas, gasoline, and food. By 22 December, 92,000 survivors had been evacuated, according to Soviet sources. In this context, the presence of foreign relief workers, who represented hope for finding additional survivors, could well have slowed the pace of evacuation.

The interior wall of a collapsed apartment building with the front door and a photograph intact.

One of the many piles of coffins awaiting burial.

Severely damaged or destroyed apartment buildings in Leninakan

with a rescue worker and survivors.

An aerial view of Leninakan.

Foreign rescue workers with two of their trained dogs.

A rescue worker trying to reach and free a survivor.

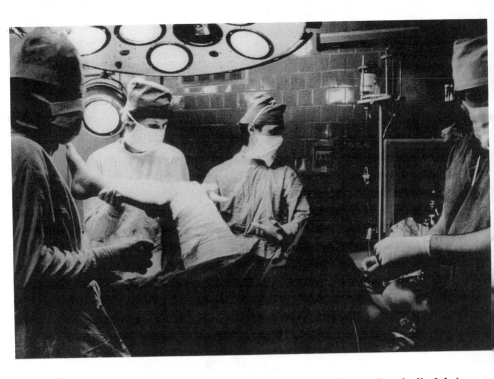

A survivor in surgery. Leninakan's hospitals were destroyed and all of their on-duty physicians and nurses perished. Survivors had to be taken to Yerevan.

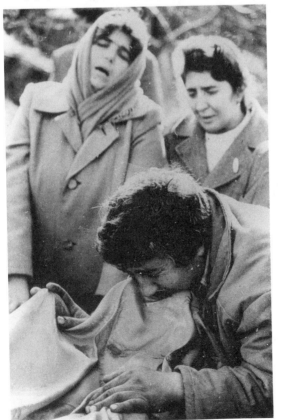

Survivors mourning a victim.

On hearing the news of the earthquake, Soviet leader Mikhail Gorbachev cut short his visit to the United States and flew to Armenia to assess the situation. He is addressing a crowd of Armenians. (Gorbachev appears on the far right, in the hat, with his wife Raisa.)

*There were large-scale protest demonstrations in Yerevan beginning in Februa[ry]
1988. The banner (top photo) calls for a special session of the Armenian parlia[ment]
to unite Moutainous Karabagh with Armenia, to organize and defend the Ar[me]-
nian people from violence, and to recognize the genocide.*

Several French relief workers were embittered by their Armenian mission. This bitterness stems from their feeling that the possibilities for aid offered by foreign nations were underutilized. There was no attempt on the part of the Soviet authorities to assist the foreign relief workers by coordinating the searches. As a result many opportunities were lost:

> For an entire afternoon Soviet officials drove around in a car with naval fire fighters from Marseilles, all the while promising to take them to sites where there were survivors. They approached one site and said, "We made a mistake, it is not here." By the end of the day, the relief workers returned, furious that they had not been able to work even once.

On the other hand, the foreign relief workers lacked heavy equipment, especially for lifting. Unable to transport such equipment by air, they were dependent on Soviet sources. There was a great need for civilian or military cranes, but neither was put at their disposal in sufficient quantities by the Soviets.

Transportation was also inadequate; this limited access to certain areas. One relief worker also had the unpleasant impression of being exploited in the mass media by Mr. Gorbachev; in reality the presence and assistance of relief workers seemed secondary to Gorbachev's major objective—to reestablish political control after 10 December.

THE KINGDOM OF DEATH

This heading is not meant to take pleasure in the morbid but to express what the relief workers and members of the private relief organizations saw. It is taken from one of the witnesses. The relief workers arrived late at the disaster sites, which contained few survival pockets and brought to light many more bodies than survivors. In the course of the conversations that make up this narrative, only a few people were able to come to terms directly with the shock they must have felt. Here is what some of them said.

Shocked Eyewitnesses

One witness, a veteran of a dozen disaster-relief campaigns, admitted to "being truly shocked by the scale of this disaster and its consequences. In Armenia it was Hell with a capital H."

This distress was caused by several factors. Not central—but also not negligible—were the difficult physical conditions that left their mark on the relief workers. Working day and night in the cold and mud with no chance to wash or rest, the relief workers were physically exhausted. In general, their fatigue did not lead to emotional outbursts or personality conflicts.

Above and beyond this first reason, the relief workers themselves suffered from emotional traumas. Thus the physicians from the French detachments held 21 consultations with relief workers suffering from fits of crying and attacks of anxiety. Working all day long with people who had nearly always lost several members of their families could not leave the workers unaffected. An Armenian diasporan relief worker confided:

> I wanted to give them some kind of moral support so I spoke with many of the survivors. But at one moment, I admitted that I could not say anything to this man. He was sitting on the rubble. We saw each other and I could not say a word. I saw the sorrow in his eyes. . . . Sometimes you can only be silent.

An Armenian woman from the diaspora who took part in the relief efforts with COSI said:

> You feel tremendous guilt when someone comes up to you and asks you to come with your dog to help their family and you have to be content to take down their name and explain that you will be there as soon as possible, maybe tomorrow.

Added to this are horrible scenes, such as mounds of children's book satchels in the wreckage of schools and the piles of coffins. This environment led a third diasporan witness to have nightmares on the rare occasions when he slept. "I saw my own children in the ruins," he said.

Another factor that added to the stress of the relief workers was the rarity of freeing buried survivors. Never had so many relief workers brought out so few survivors. Although it was not a question of their competence, how can we not understand their disappointment? One relief worker said:

> The first day we hoped to find many survivors. We worked at a factory that had collapsed on 300 workers. We found nothing but bodies, not one survivor.

A second example of false hope occurred one week after the earthquake during a live report on the 8 p.m. news. This was at a work site next to the plateau of Antenna 2 (television). A witness recounts the events:

> Survivors had been found on this spot during the first two days. Then only bodies, 120, had been removed. But some time before the program, newly arrived Czech rescue workers spotted a survival zone in between two large concrete slabs; this opened the possibility of survivors. On the ground a man of about sixty and his son, members of a family that lived in the apartment, would come and go between the charcoal brazier at the foot of the ruins and the survival zone, looking anxious and hopeful at the same time. At their request, the television team agreed to leave their lights on to help rescuers after completing the news report. At 1 a.m. when the father and son came down and went toward the pile of coffins, everyone knew their family had not survived.

The third and last example of disappointed hope: for several days rescuers had located a woman thanks to her radio. During the search, an interpreter established contact, but they were not successful in precisely locating her and could not save her.

The mammoth scale of the disaster and the small number of survivors led one witness to feel "ridiculous" for attempting to help. He said:

> The first night I wanted to run away. I asked myself, "But what are we doing here in this chaos, in this void?" In the end I got over it, because we wanted to do all we could to save people, even if it was only one life.

This choice was rewarded when a team brought out a survivor. "Then," said a rescue worker, "we would burst into tears." This fit of crying, which expressed a freedom from anxiety and a real sense of satisfaction, only lasted a short time.

Confronted by a test of such magnitude, people protected themselves to the best of their ability. One relief worker deliberately avoided looking at corpses so he could conserve his strength to aid the survivors, while others gained strength by reading about disasters. Another made it a point to focus on only one small aspect of the larger drama, so as not to be totally overwhelmed by the scope of it.

The scale of the catastrophe, the eerie appearance of the city (as though it had been bombed), the concentration of horror, and the ineffectiveness of people to alter the consequences shook more than one eyewitness to his philosophical foundations. One witness said:

> The power of fate was bought home to me. That nature would play a hand in a major political crisis between the Armenians and the central government is beyond our comprehension. Even if I am convinced that it was natural, the earthquake couldn't have happened at a worse time for the Armenians. There are times when fate is too eloquent. There are times when, if I were a believer, I would respond as the Armenians do by saying, "God has abandoned us." [3]

Another eyewitness explained:

> When I arrived in Leninakan, I was terribly shocked.

Death had imposed His law by taking tens of thousands of lives within several minutes. It was the Kingdom of Death. I was at a great King's court. It was a majestic moment in the sense that it did not belong to man; it was the Gods who reigned. That is why people's actions seemed almost blasphemous. They intruded on a history that was not of their making. The scene reminded us of the frailty of our human condition. In a certain sense our actions resembled an exorcism. The earthquake constantly reminded us of our condition, and we wanted to escape it. We wanted to take the initiative from the Gods by rescuing a few survivors before death carried them off. But Death was there. You could feel His presence, like a depressing grip. On every corner soldiers, as though they were the servants of Death, unloaded and piled up the coffins with sparse, utilitarian movements, at once casual, relaxed and resigned to the task and potentially threatening. Dozens, hundreds of coffins . . . in every corner of the rescue area.

Around the charcoal heaters, the survivors and the rescuers warmed themselves. It was cold and humid and there was mud everywhere. At this time of year night came quickly; the floodlights lit the rescue sites, the cranes, and the people. The light was not dazzling but reflected menacingly through the fog. Movement seemed abrupt and jerky in this light. From time to time several men came out of the ruins. They went to look for coffins: they had pulled out one, two, three, four, ten bodies. There was something sacrilegious in gazing on these gnarled bodies, each wrapped in a shroud and placed in a coffin.

Death was no longer an allegory but an omnipresent reality. The vision was apocalyptic.

By virtue of its scale, this catastrophe entered world history and would remain a part of it, much like Pompei. It was a historic event, a reference point for people who would reflect upon it and say, "I was there, I made my mark on history," much like an astronaut walking on the moon. For the first time in my life I was a witness to history. I was a participant at that moment coming face to face with the tragic destiny of humanity.

In a certain sense, it was my good fortune to see and live what will be recorded in books. This vision of the human condition will be with me till the day I die.

At the same time that the rescuers were traumatized by the catastrophe, they felt that they should be there. Many gave the impression of being truly fulfilled. For example, one of the witnesses said:

I saw a diasporan Armenian walking toward the survivors of a village carrying an armful of blankets. He was transformed and exalted by his good deeds. I had the impression that this moment had been the goal of his mission and achieving it had erased all of the difficulties he had experienced.

Two witnesses described an Armenian diasporan relief worker who "was clearly very upset by the experience yet he remained strong and at the same time feigned detachment, much like a poet of the event."

If everyone had been marked in some way by their presence in the disaster sites, how did the diasporan Armenians in particular live the experience? All of them were aware that this was their chance to carry out and express urgent feelings they had from the moment the disaster became public: to bring aid to Armenians in distress. With one exception, all of them felt a high degree of brotherhood with the Armenians of the homeland.

Their Armenian identity was revived and strengthened and the dual identity of the third generation reinforced. Their return to France was not always simple. Some of them wanted time to reflect upon and "digest" their experience before sharing it with others. All of them felt it was their duty to bear witness to what had happened, but many had great difficulty talking with their families about their experiences because they were aware of how much suffering their descriptions would cause.

The Importance of Foreign Aid

Foreign aid cannot be measured solely in terms of the number of lives saved. As one witness expressed it, "The Armenians need to cry with others." The relief effort demonstrated that they were not abandoned, neither by the diaspora nor by foreign countries. While the survivors drew strength from one and all, the solidarity of the diaspora seemed "normal" to them. For this reason they were even more deeply touched by foreign assistance, especially the French. Foreign aid had great symbolic importance above and beyond its material accomplishments.

NOTES

1. *Liberation*, 15 December 1988.

2. This same Friday, 16 December, according to *Le Monde* dated 18 December, the rescue workers, whose nationality was not clearly identified, rescued three people in Leninakan who were saved by being in an elevator cage at the time of the earthquake.

3. In Baku, the Azeris congratulated themselves on the occasion of the "punishment inflicted by Allah" on the Armenians. *Le Monde*, 11 December 1988.

CHAPTER 4

The Disaster Victims

Soviet authorities were in agreement with foreign witnesses that the number of disaster victims was between 500,000 and 700,000, or about 60 percent of the people in the disaster zones and 19 percent of Armenians in Soviet Armenia.

Private relief organizations from abroad did all that they could to provide assistance to these people. They began arriving in Armenia on Saturday, 10 December 1988, and they remained for several weeks after the return of the rescue workers. Some, like Doctors without Borders, remained for nearly a year.

A TRAUMATIZED POPULATION

On their arrival, Doctors without Borders found survivors in a state of shock, their faces fixed in horror, walking about with no purpose in mind, looking for their dead as well as for possible survivors, and managing to retain a certain dignity in their pain.

Their faces fixed in horror, walking about with no purpose in mind...

As one witness recalled:

The first few days I remained in Yerevan to work in the hospitals. Although I hadn't gone to Leninakan, the faces of the survivors spoke eloquently to me. It was an expression that had witnessed horror, that had witnessed the end of the world. When I went to Leninakan several days later, I did not see anything I hadn't known from my first impressions of the survivors' faces. On my return to France, I could not stand to look at the photos taken by my friends. That same expression was there.

Another woman said:

This look was the result of a general condition among the survivors. Their whole insides were locked tight, frozen, while they were nevertheless moving around. They had not recovered from the earthquake.

Two other witnesses added that "In the days following the disaster the survivors lived by their survival instincts alone, without even being hungry." Many were nonfunctional, wandering from one end of the town to the other, totally lost, often haunted by feelings of guilt, "Why am I alive while my family is dead?"

Everyone was preoccupied with rescuing survivors still buried under the rubble and finding the deceased, but most of the survivors were too traumatized and too poorly trained to take part in any really efficient rescue efforts. Doctors without Borders often encountered difficulties in motivating people to take part in rescue operations:

In the village of Gularak, only one survivor helped us to put up our tent, which we would use to store our supplies and equipment.

There were others, though, who put themselves at the disposal of private relief organizations or presented a plan for joint action as a last resort. One of the directors of Doctors without Borders said:

> I came across a man who had been wandering about for several days. He heard me speak French and began speaking with me. He was a French teacher and had been buried underneath his school. He survived but lost his wife and two children.

> We didn't have translators and I asked him to join our team. This made him feel useful, and little by little Martin Pachaian took back his will to live. His excellent knowledge of the country was a great help to us.

Another witness explained that:

> Other survivors hid in their work to avoid having to think about their dead. Our chauffeur was one of those. He lost eighteen members of his family.

When the body of a family member was brought up, the survivors often gave the impression of not recognizing that he or she was dead. Others continued to speak to or about this person as though he or she were alive. Still others would list their dead without any visible emotion. One witness recalled:

> A dozen people were gathered in front of the ruins of a six-story building. A woman told me in a cold, distant voice, "My children and my husband are dead under there." She then brought over a 12-year-old boy with a dazed expression. "His parents and sister are dead." Wanting to say something to comfort her, I said, "The diaspora and international aid will do what they can to help you." They were moved, but I felt ridiculous, of no help at all.

Looking for their dead as well as for possible survivors . . .

The survivors made every effort to reclaim their loved ones and to provide them with a decent burial in order to pay their last respects and so that the bodies would not remain anonymous. A witness provided examples:

A dazed mother, with the shoe of her child in one hand, walked painfully among the ruins. As she came upon the body of a child, she would stop and try on the shoe, hoping in this way to identify her loved one.[1]

This search for the "missing" was important to the point that survivors sometimes refused to "lose time" in caring for themselves. There was one young man who refused surgery because he had not been able to find his wife's body and give her a proper burial.

This search for bodies went on for twenty days after the earthquake. This need to provide a proper burial for the dead is shared by all cultures, but it took on a special significance for the Armenians, given their history. The Armenians could not retrieve or bury the victims of the genocide. In 1988 the search for the missing sought to prevent a similar fate for the earthquake victims.

The genocide and the earthquake are distinct in the sense that one is a political event and the other a natural one, but at the same time they are linked by the fact that the majority of victims were lost forever. As a disaporan Armenian explained:

On 7 December 1988, our community once again lost victims without identities, victims who "disappeared" under tons of concrete. The concept of "disappearance" recurs too often in Armenian history: the disappearance of half of the Armenians of the Ottoman Empire during the genocide, the majority of victims of the earthquake, the destruction of the city of Spitak. . . . The disappearance raises the possibility of a failure to recognize the tragedy by non-Armenians. That would bring additional pain to the community. For that reason we feel strongly that the meaning of the events of 7 December 1988 should be recorded in history.

Maintaining a certain dignity in their pain . . .

The eyewitness accounts are in agreement that after the

earthquake, survivors as well as residents of Yerevan put their political aspirations on hold to devote their energies to delivering assistance. There are no eyewitness accounts of Armenians coordinating activities to exploit the disaster for political ends.

Above and beyond this moral sense, the dignity of the Armenians faced with tragedy impressed the witnesses. In particular, when they were with foreign relief workers who were not diasporan Armenians, the survivors made special efforts not to burden the relief workers with their pain and their losses. They tried to maintain their dignity. When they could no longer contain themselves and they let their emotions go, they would quickly recover. As one witness reported:

> I remember Martin Pachaian. This man always remained very composed and dignified. While we quickly understood that we should avoid speaking with the survivors of the probable losses in their families, the conversation unintentionally struck that theme. His mouth tightened and his eyes filled with tears. "I lost my wife and my two children," he blurted out as he left the room. In half a minute he was back, once again composed and dignified. He almost apologized for letting go.

A second witness reported:

> In the village of Stepanavan, the natural leader of the community held on to his dignity and honor above all else. When we offered him blankets, he refused. And he ordered a man who laughed nervously, "Calm down, present a good image of yourself."

A third witness recalled:

> Parents who were lucky enough to have one or several surviving children found the strength to continue the struggle for them.

Many drew the strength to persevere from their faith. Two other witnesses said:

One night a family invited us to dinner. While they were recounting their losses, and were reflecting upon this new misfortune, the head of the family left the room and returned with an old Bible dating from the early nineteenth century. All of them made the sign of the cross. "Here is our hope," he said as he displayed the book. "Faith will allow us to overcome this new catastrophe."

The survivors went out of their way to welcome those who had come from abroad to help them. The reception went beyond the traditional hospitality of these people to reveal the symbolic importance of international solidarity. The coordinator for Doctors without Borders in Leninakan described his experience:

> For the first three weeks we were there, everything was free. The Armenians refused to accept as much as a single rouble. They offered us everything we needed: food, drink, lodging, gasoline, transportation. . . . Each day, as though by some miracle, they managed to come up with food for thirty-five people.

On numerous occasions humanitarian volunteers from abroad were invited to eat and sleep over with local families. One of these relief workers recalled his experiences:

> One night around 11 p.m., after a day of consultations, we decided to take a little rest. When we started to spread out our sleeping bags in the dispensary, the Armenian interpreters exclaimed, "You're going to sleep here! Wait, we'll go look for cars to take you to our homes." Twenty minutes later, they came back with several vehicles and took all fifteen of us in the team to their families. At each home we were warmly welcomed.

> They freely deprived themselves of all their provisions to lay out a beautiful table of food. Without ever losing sight of the circumstances, Armenians and non-Armenians went through some emotional moments in learning

about one another amid toasts to "international aid," "Armenia," and "Karabakh. . . ."

The Armenians asked the non-Armenians about their knowledge of the political movement during the months preceding the earthquake and probed diasporan Armenians on the possibility of maintaining their Armenian identity outside of the motherland. Everyone expressed the hope that, at a minimum, the earthquake would lead to ties between Armenia and the outside world.

The past, present, and future of Armenia and the diaspora were the topic of passionate discussions. But despite the warm welcome, each person, from time to time, withdrew into him- or herself because of the depth of the tragedy that surrounded them.

Those present also sometimes recalled the missing. The guests then learned that an integral part of the family was deceased. In a sort of exorcism through speech, each evoked his or her deceased in the company of other members of this fraternity, in a ritual of collective mourning.

During the evenings or at meetings, several witnesses were asked individually about a rumor that was circulating in the days after the disaster: "The earthquake was caused by the Soviet government, for example, by means of an underground explosion." One of the witnesses related that:

> One evening an Armenian brought up this idea of a staged earthquake. He favored the idea of an underground nuclear explosion. "If that were the case," I answered, "it would have been recorded at monitoring stations outside the country. Armenia is situated in an earthquake zone and has always known earthquakes." An Armenian physician then said "You're right, but the earthquake came at too opportune a time for the Soviets for it not to have been set off." If an educated man

insists on believing this, then it is clear that—whether right or wrong—the concept of a deliberately planned earthquake will henceforth be a part of the Armenian collective unconscious. It has taken root because the earthquake occurred in the midst of a full-blown political crisis.

This is the case, despite the fact that the Karabagh Committee "tirelessly explained to groups and individuals the absurdity of these suspicions that the earthquake was deliberately set." [2] The author himself contacted a French seismologist, who confirmed that "no underground nuclear explosion could achieve the magnitude of the 7 December 1988 earthquake."

ASSISTANCE BY DWB TO THE VICTIMS

After landing in Yerevan on 11 December at 7 a.m., Doctors without Borders split into two teams. One remained in Yerevan, the Armenian capital, to assist in the hospitals, while the other took the road to Leninakan, hoping to participate in the care of survivors who had been rescued from the rubble. DWB was authorized to proceed to Leninakan because of the prior relationship between the French-Armenian surgeons in DWB and the Armenian Minister of Health.

Arriving from France full of hope that they could save the injured and the trapped who were seriously hurt, all had to adapt to a situation that was different from what they had imagined. By this Sunday—now four days after the catastrophe—the seriously wounded had already perished and trapped survivors were the exception. They overcame their disappointment and responded to the pressing need of the moment: to care for the survivors by replacing the destroyed health clinics with general medical dispensaries.

Opening Dispensaries in Leninakan

During the first three weeks after their arrival, Doctors without Borders opened three dispensaries.

On Monday, 12 December 1988, they opened the first one in a pharmacy located in the center of the city, at Kirov Place. The main room, about 30 square meters (323 square feet), was soon divided into four consultation sections by using survival blankets. Although very narrow, each section did allow for the intimacy necessary for a medical consultation. Each cubicle had what was needed to conduct an examination for the patient: blood-pressure cuff, stethoscope, and the like.

In order to protect the patients from the cold, DWB arranged for a waiting room at the entrance. They stocked their medicines on the premises in a 15-square-meter (161 square feet) area next to the dispensary. The dispensary opened its doors at the end of the day and was immediately successful. They took care of 150 people the first day.

Beginning on Tuesday the 13th, Doctors without Borders worked in shifts in order to handle the 350 to 400 patients they were seeing daily. Diasporan Armenians in DWB were very active in the dispensaries, eliminating some of the language difficulties.

The first dispensary was overwhelmed by demand, and Doctors without Borders decided to open a second one on Friday, 16 December, in a two-story building that had been a day-care center. Logistical specialists from the organization laid out the space so that about thirty patients could be accommodated for long-term care. To make this possible, they built a "living space" on the second floor, consisting of a dormitory, a kitchen, a shower with hot water, and an administrative office, all heated by a stove. On the first floor, they set up a waiting room and consultation rooms that were also heated.

Thanks to a generator, they were able to construct a small operating room equipped with its own independent lighting source. These arrangements were not completed until Sunday the 18th, but the operating room opened on the 16th for the care of one survivor from the ruins (the patient Anahide). Consultations began on Saturday the 17th.

On 1 January 1989, Doctors without Borders opened its third dispensary. In addition to these three dispensaries, care was provided in the villages by mobile dispensaries, and in some instances at patients' homes.

Care for victims would not have been so effective without the tremendous wealth of experience DWB has accrued in the areas of supply and logistics. As one of the DWB heads explained:

> Our organization was founded eighteen years ago by experienced medical field workers who understood that a medical team could not be effective without having all the materials necessary for true autonomy.
>
> Therefore, we took Soviet-manufactured automobiles, Ladas, with us on the first plane leaving for Armenia so that our teams could move about freely. We chose that particular brand specifically so that any needed repairs could be done on the spot. As another example, we put together fifty special medical and non-medical kits to respond to specific disaster-related problems such as the need to provide lighting. The lighting kits consisted of a generator, electrical wires, extension cords, outlet strips, neon bulbs, candles, and oil . . . necessary materials that allow a team to be immediately operational under any conditions.
>
> We also wanted the medicines to be easily usable. Each was tried out beforehand and labeled according to its international pharmaceutical name—not by any one of its countless commercial labels. Communications between the teams and the Paris headquarters were also planned so as to minimize the loss of time, energy, and money that results from incorrect information. Teams were also busy, of course, in attending to the survivors by installing heated tents and distributing hot plates, blankets, and clothes. . . . All of this adds up to supporting life and slowly getting things moving again.
>
> Disaster relief teams are not only made up of physicians but also of logistical staff. They know how to maintain a car as well as a dispensary, and they can deal with administrative problems, decontaminate water, and reestablish radio communications.

One witness, a diasporan Armenian who teamed up with DWB in Leninakan for the first time, recalled:

> being very impressed by the independence and self assurance made possible by the logistical support staff. It provided Doctors without Borders with an efficiency that is unrivaled.

Medical Consultations in the DWB Dispensaries

The large number of survivors who came to the dispensaries did not only come to be cared for. They wanted to meet the people who had come from abroad to help them. Except for the 1 to 5 percent who required surgery, most of the consultations should be seen as "calls for help." Most often the health problem predated the earthquake, and it allowed the patients to directly or indirectly express their loss of family and the pain caused by the cataclysm.

Only 25 percent of the consultations concerned problems directly related to the earthquake. The days and nights spent outdoors in the cold caused many cases of pneumonia, bronchitis, flu, sore throats, tonsilitis, and all of the accompanying symptoms. While some of these problems did not appear to be very serious, they could lead to complications if left untreated, especially in children. As one of the physicians explained:

> These consultations covered extended care for patients who received emergency care under less than fully antiseptic conditions, which led to festering wounds, abscesses, and even gangrene. We had to treat numerous patients with massive antibiotic dosages, which they had not received because of the lack of medicines. In the course of our treatment, we discovered several serious diagnostic errors such as plastering over open fractures, which caused gangrene. This would have led directly to amputation or even to the patient's death if we hadn't intervened.

Finally, Doctors without Borders carried out several operations under general anesthesia, notably for the removal of scar tissue and necrosis.

In 75 percent of the cases, consultations began with an examination for a condition that predated the earthquake and had sometimes been aggravated by the trauma of the disaster. The eight problem areas below were the most common:

1. Problems of the lower legs: e.g., varicose veins, phlebitis, arterial difficulties.
2. Vascular abnormalities: e.g., hemorrhoids.
3. Urological and kidney deficiencies: e.g., kidney and gall stones, renal colic, pilonephritis, poor kidney function.
4. Digestive problems: e.g., ulcers, gastritis.
5. Lower torso problems: e.g., lumbago, sciatica.
6. Cardiac problems: e.g., high blood pressure, heart trouble.
7. Diabetes.
8. Tooth decay.

As a result of these consultations, Doctors without Borders became aware of the low level of general health among the Armenians. The absence of a balanced diet, preventative health care, and quality medical care—in conjunction with excessive alcohol and tobacco intake—led to a gradual but premature aging. This situation led one physician to speculate as to whether the real emergency was caused by the earthquake or the poor state of the people's health prior to the earthquake.

While speaking with doctors from abroad, the Armenians often expressed their doubts concerning the competence of Soviet doctors whom they accused as well of ignoring those who were unable to pay them "under the table" for health services.

After several unfortunate experiences, Doctors without Borders decided not to ask the patients about their family's deceased members. But often after having discussed their own chronic health problems, one-third of the consultations ended with the patients speaking spontaneously about their personal tragedies. One physician referred to "opening the gates to repressed tears" and "to people coming undone."

One woman burst out, "I lost my children and my husband. The building collapsed on them while I was out at the bakery buying the bread I forgot the night before." A man wept, "My son was on leave from the army, and I found him dead under the stones!" A woman unburdened herself, "I saw my daughter in the morning. We had breakfast together. She was home from the university and she is dead."

The physicians tried to comfort these people. After they quickly regained their composure, these survivors left with their dignity intact.

Sometimes—although very rarely—the doctors learned of a "miraculous" story. In one family of six, for example, all survived: the father was the only one rescued from his factory, the mother and one of the children had time to flee their building, and the three other children were part of small group of survivors at their school.

The dispensaries became places where one could "speak one's pain." This opened the way to the process of mourning and to eventually lessening that pain.

During the course of their consultations beginning on Friday, 16 December, doctors noticed the appearance and development of various anguished states among the patients. These were expressed as chronic terror, insomnia, nightmares, bedwetting, impotence, and menstrual irregularities. The onset of these symptoms coincided (not by accident) with the departure of the foreign rescue workers, which signaled the end of hope and the start of collective mourning.

This psychological process gathered momentum as the following measures were taken: beginning of the cleanup of the ruins on Tuesday, 20 December; start of the dynamiting of badly damaged buildings on Thursday, 22 December; and the burial of the last coffins from Wednesday the 21st to Friday the 30th. On about 25 December, the physicians began to see the first cases of serious psychological deterioration. A psychiatrist reported:

a woman singing and dancing out her mourning during the night next to the graves in the cemetery. She had lost contact with other people and hurled out words without constructing sentences: "Children!" "Tombs!" "Sky!" "Houses!"

This same doctor saw:

a man who heard his pregnant daughter from beneath the ruins for three days. He had accidently caused her safety area to collapse while trying to bring her help.

He was only able to bring out her body, still warm. The poor man was delirious by now and acting out auditory and visual hallucinations. He pretended to be a king and/or queen, receiving presents from the masses. Lifting up his bedsheets, he said he saw animals coming and going and announced that he was in combat with them.

How did children respond to the disaster? First of all, because of the poor construction of many schools and the timing of the earthquake, few children survived. Fifteen thousand children perished in Leninakan alone.

The witnesses met few youngsters and remarked that they met more parents "orphaned" from their children than actual orphans. The few children who survived were kept at home by their relatives to avoid any kind of accident from dense traffic, or they were evacuated away from the dangers of the disaster zones. The few children encountered by our witnesses did not give the impression of reacting like the adults. They were living more for the moment than in the past. They met one girl of twelve who was caring for the rest of the family.

This does not alter the fact that the children, like the adults, will be marked for life by this catastrophe. One witness, an Armenian doctor from the diaspora, suggested that:

this collective tragedy will mark the Armenians, including the diaspora, for at least three generations, following the model of the genocide of 1915, which they still mourn today.

Whether a divine sign or a self-induced one, after feeling abandoned by God, there were repeated reports of visions of the Virgin Mary around 25 December several kilometers from Yerevan.

Doctors without Borders: The Long-Range Program

Several days after their arrival, Doctors without Borders took charge of part of the distribution of donations by people and organizations around the world; clothes and foodstuffs and the administration of stocks of medicines and medical supplies.

After 25 December 1988, they devoted themselves to the long-term care of the survivors and brought a number of programs into action during 1989. Assistance with the distribution of clothes and tents and the sorting of medical donations went on for several months in order to derive the maximum benefit from international aid.

In cooperation with Handicap International, Doctors without Borders launched a physical therapy program for the injured, especially for amputees. These two organizations will ensure that a portion of those in need of artificial limbs will receive them. According to Soviet figures the number is 400.

To put the 80 artificial kidneys that arrived from abroad to the best possible use, DWB trained local physicians in dialysis in order to develop this specialization locally. In response to serious shortcomings in Soviet pediatric medicine, DWB developed an infant resuscitation program in cooperation with hospital physicians in Lyons, France. Before this program was created, a minimum of one infant a day was dying in Yerevan due to repiratory distress.

To help maintain the health of the surviving population, DWB distributed thousands of "family hygiene kits." These were packaged in a bag and designed to provide for the needs of a family of ten. Each kit contained toothpaste, toothbrushes, soap, cotton, wash cloths, towels, and combs.

At the close of this chapter, which is dedicated to the survivors, we should examine an allegation that appeared in the

French press during the month of December 1988: "Soviet coordination of foreign aid to the victims was deficient." [3] Do the eyewitnesses confirm this observation or not?

A specialist in disaster studies observed: "It is in the nature of major disasters that social structures will be disorganized at least for some period of time." Also, the object of the question is not whether there was disorganization but how long it lasted.

In France, during the recent devastating floods at Nîmes, the breakdown period before reorganization was two days.

In Armenia, at what moment did the witnesses see evidence of Soviet coordination of foreign relief efforts for the survivors? All witnesses agree that there were deficiencies in the Soviet coordination efforts on behalf of foreign relief programs for the survivors during the entire period considered here, i.e., through 7 January 1989. By that date, the authorities had not taken charge of aid to survivors, having in fact abandoned them to the foreigners.

Before specifying the disadvantages of this situation, we should recognize one advantage: the relative freedom of action enjoyed by the private foreign relief agencies who were able to put their autonomy to good use. However, inadequate Soviet coordination of foreign relief efforts (which was rightfully their responsibility) did damage the overall efficiency of the international aid effort.

The absence of competent and motivated official support personnel impeded the decision-making process. The behavior of the bureaucrats in charge of donations from the international community, along with the improper assessment of real needs and their communication to the outside world, slowed down the distribution of goods and services.

Late and illogical measures to control access to the disaster areas also caused bottlenecks on the roads and long delays in travel time between Leninakan and Yerevan. This was especially damaging during the ten days following the earthquake, when communication links had not yet been established. Thus it took two days for Doctors without Borders to receive the materials they lacked from their warehouses in Yerevan.

And finally, how could we not mention the authorities' refusal to lend a helicopter to Doctors without Borders on Monday, 12 December? This would have allowed for a much quicker estimate of losses, damage, and needs, especially in the villages.

NOTES

1. *Liberation*, 14 December 1988.
2. Telegram from Raphael Ghazarian, member of the Karabagh Committee, to the editor and chief of *Kommunist*.
3. *Le Monde*, 17 December 1988.

PART III

THE
POLITICAL
DIMENSION

CHAPTER 5

The Earthquake
in Its
Historical Context

The earthquake on 7 December 1988 occurred in the midst of a major political conflict between the Armenians and the Soviet state, giving the earthquake an altogether unique quality. The unrest preceding the earthquake was reported in the French press as having two dimensions: Armenian national aspirations and their demand for the reunification of Mountainous Karabagh with the Republic of Armenia. In order to understand why Armenian demands cannot be reduced to the level of nationalism, we will begin by placing Armenian national aspirations and territorial claims into a broader perspective.

These two dimensions in Armenian history are not recent phenomena; they have their roots in earlier decades, even in preceding centuries. Since the nineteenth century (and particularly after the 1915 genocide) nationalism has been a preoccupation among Armenians. This understandable obsession with "biological survival, identity, and nationality" has shaped behavior in Armenia and in the diaspora. It explains the sacrifice of national independence by the Republic of Armenia in 1920 in favor of Soviet protection in order to escape the assault of a new offensive by the Kemalist Turks.[1] This republic and its red, blue, and orange tricolor flag are central reference points up to this very day.

If the Sovietization of Armenia protected the Armenians from the Turks for a long time, this did not occur without violence or feelings of national frustration. The brutality of Sovietization first provoked an anti-Soviet uprising on 18 February 1921, which the Bolsheviks put down after several months.

In 1921 the Soviet regime refused to reunify a territory with an Armenian majority with the Republic of Armenia. This territory, Karabagh—its Turkish name—was given the status of an autonomous region and attached to the Republic of Azerbaijan, populated primarily by Shi'ite Moslem Turks (see the political map of the Caucasus).

In 1923, the Karabagh region, which had been reduced to its mountainous core, was set up as the "Autonomous Region of Mountainous Karabagh." With an area of 4,388 square kilometers (1,694 square miles), its capital has been Stepanagert since 1923. At the time the region was 94 percent Armenian. In 1988 the region had a total population of 180,000, of which 75 percent were Armenian. The rest of the inhabitants were Turks.

Seeing that their identity was threatened, the Armenians of Mountainous Karabagh have long demanded reunification with Soviet Armenia. Armenian territorial claims date from the earliest days of Sovietization, and they have been continuously fed by a frustrated Armenian nationalism.

The union of Mountainous Karabagh with Azerbaijan is not the only legacy of Sovietization. First, all references to the genocide were forbidden from 1920 to 1965. Second, the totalitarian nature of Soviet rule led to a fragmentation of society. Third, the regime had no success in achieving its objective of "ethnic symbiosis."[2] Finally, the intensive industrialization of Armenia gave rise to major environmental problems.

Historians note the reassertion of Armenian national aspirations and their crystallization around the question of Karabagh reunification each time that there was a change in the leadership of central state power. In effect, this issue represented a synthesis of all aspects of the Armenian national problem: Karabagh is attached to Azerbaijan (which represents the traditional enemy Turkey), the population is exposed to various pressures and forced to migrate, the question of cultural survival is acute, and economic problems are legion.

Thus a movement for the reunification of Karabagh appeared in the decade of the 1920s as an expression of the New Economic Policy (NEP). In the aftermath of the bloody Stalinist decades, there was a slow reassertion of Armenian history, beginning under Khrushchev, in the period from 1955 to 1961.

In 1965, the fiftieth anniversary of the genocide marked an important turning point: 100,000 to 150,000 Armenian demonstrators demanded recognition of the genocide and the recovery of their lands. An Armenian national movement began to emerge, and it specified Karabagh and the protection of Armenian national monuments as top priorities.

During the second half of the 1960s, the Soviet state granted several symbolic concessions, including a monument in commemoration of the genocide, but the Armenians of Mountainous Karabagh continued to be denied the reunification of their region with Armenia.

After Gorbachev came to power in 1985, observers noted the refusal of local authorities to submit to the orders of the central government, and an evolution in the controls exercised over speech among part of the population. A television program concerning the Armenian language, a denunciation of the unification of Mountainous Karabagh with Azerbaijan (a semi-veiled critique of Stalinism), and an ecological movement (arising from people's concerns about environmental degradation and the operation of a nuclear power plant not far from Yerevan in an earthquake zone) appeared in Armenia.

1987 TO 25 MARCH 1988:
FROM ECOLOGY TO *NYET* BY WAY OF KARABAGH

Two movements developed and came to light during the first half of 1987. They concerned Mountainous Karabagh and the First Secretary of the Armenian Communist Party.

On 5 March 1987, Souren Aiyvazian (a member of the Communist Party), sent a letter to Gorbachev in which he demanded the reunification of Mountainous Karabagh with Armenia. Another sign of a developing new wave of demands over territory and identity was the April reedition of a book dedicated to the Armenian monuments in Karabagh. It called attention to the alarming rate of deterioration of the monuments, while at the same time implicitly establishing Armenian rights to the land.

During the month of June, the First Secretary of the Party in Armenia, Karen Demirchian (nicknamed "The Little King" by the Armenians) was harshly criticized during a Party session. Since Demirchian had refused to follow Gorbachev's directives on reform, Gorbachev seemed to be looking for a way to end his tenure in office and launched a harsh attack on him. The goal of the Secretary General was to "legitimize" Demirchian's replacement by a more loyal follower.

What precipitated the crisis, which up till now had remained dormant, was the publication of an alarmist article in the official journal *Literaturnaia Gazeta* on the topic of dangerous pollutants emitted by chemical plants in Yerevan. The author, Zori Balayan, a member of the Communist Party, provided an apocalyptic vision of the situation and attacked the local authorities. He presented the local party heads as a veritable mafia with no concern whatsoever for the health of the public. An expert analyzed this article as a maneuver by the central authorities to provoke a popular uprising against the local authorities, which would be the pretext for their removal.

Whatever may have been the case, the Armenians felt that their "biological survival" was threatened, and they soon became alarmed in large numbers.

A scientific commission was immediately sent from Moscow to investigate appropriate measures to be taken. The commission was content merely to recommend closing half of a synthetic rubber plant by the following September 1st. (Actually, this part of the factory was already inoperative, but the people did not know it.) During that entire summer, ecological and territorial petitions were circulated. On 1 September, the Armenians gathered in front of the factory to verify that the recommendation was being carried out. They saw the chimneys continuing to spew forth fumes, which in reality were coming from the second section of the plant. Outraged and concerned, the people immediately began large-scale demonstrations.

After several weeks, the territorial demand was added in a more explicit way to the environmental demands. The demand for the reunification of Mountainous Karabagh with the Republic of Armenia gained force when high-level party figures took a stand in favor. For example, the journalist Zori Balayan, Sergei Mikoyan, and Abel Aghanbegian (Mr. Gorbachev's economic adviser) came out in favor of reunification.

Imagining that they were "in favor" with the government, the Armenians began to hope. In January 1988 there was an air of optimism in Yerevan. Perhaps Mr. Gorbachev was going to accept this long-standing Armenian demand and break with a decades-long "colonial" approach to the question. Portraits of the Secretary General were displayed at rallies. An expert attributes this shift in demands to maneuvering by the central government. The central government realized that it could no longer control ecological anxieties, and as a result it voluntarily shifted demands to territorial matters, hoping to find them more manageable, even though there was the risk of inter-ethnic conflict and violence.

Whatever the case, the hope of a near-term reunification of Mountainous Karabagh began to grow among the Armenians, giving birth to the reemergence of the open expression of Armenian national identity. At this time the overwhelming majority of Armenians did not indulge themselves in any vision of political independence. Payruir Airikyan,[*] the long-standing militant Armenian nationalist who had formed the Union of National Self-Determination in October, was still a marginal figure.

In January of 1988, after the authorities rejected the much-hoped-for reunification for the first time, the Armenians

---

[*] *Translator's note:* Payruir Airikyan was an early and vocal advocate of an independent Armenia, separate from the Soviet Union. He spent nearly twenty years in Soviet prisons and labor camps for his activities. Airikyan has received substantial support in the West from such reactionary political figures as Senator Jesse Helms (R–NC).

of Mountainous Karabagh changed their tactics. On 12 and 13 February 1988, the district councils of Mountainous Karabagh adopted a resolution that called for a meeting of the Regional Council of Deputies of Mountainous Karabagh for the purpose of examining the issue of reunification. On the 21st, this council voted in favor of reunification by a large majority, providing a legal basis for Armenian demands.

Meanwhile, the popular movement for reunification took a big step forward. An Armenian delegation in Moscow presented "an appeal to the tsar" for reunification based on a local referendum. They returned empty-handed on 18 February. This caused an uproar, and strikes and demonstrations began in Stepanagert.

The protests began at a significant and symbolic moment— 18 February 1988 was the anniversary of 21 February 1921, the date of the creation of the Committee of Public Safety in Armenia, which rose against Bolshevik power. Revolted by the brutalities of Sovietization, this committee wanted to expel the Soviets from Armenia.

On 19 February 1988, news of a new rejection by Moscow arrived in Yerevan during a demonstration opposing the opening of a chemical plant. Quickly the territorial demand was added to the ecological demand. These historic demonstrations lasted until 26 February, bringing together nearly a million people on some days.

On 20 February, Mr. Gorbachev gave an audience to a delegation of "recognized patriots," composed of the Armenian correspondent for *Literaturnaia Gazeta*, Zori Balayan, and the poetess Sylva Kapuitikian.

During the demonstrations from 19 to 26 February, the Armenians moved daily from a nationalism of frustration to a nationalism of pride and dignity. The demonstrators lived those days as if they were experiencing a true resurrection. The solidarity of the people at that time burst through any residual fear the people had of the regime.

The Karabagh Committee in its first phase emerged during these days. It was directed by fifteen people, some of whom had close ties to the government, including Victor Hambardzoumian, Igor Mouradian, and Vazguen Manoukian.

After Tass branded these peaceful demonstrations on 23 February as "violations of public order provoked by irresponsible extremists," Mr. Gorbachev played for time. On 26 February he asked people to give him a one-month respite to develop a position. Hopeful that they had been understood, the Armenians suspended their demonstrations and made an appointment for 26 March.

Anti-Armenian massacres during 27–29 February 1988 suddenly introduced tragedy into events that had been peaceful up until then. Several dozen Armenians (and perhaps several hundred according to sources close to the Committee) were murdered by Azerbaijanis in the industrial city of Sumgait. This dormitory city of 200,000, located north of Baku in the Republic of Azerbaijan, had an Armenian community of 18,000.

During the night of 27 February hundreds of Azerbaijanis equipped with a variety of weapons and flammable liquids tortured, raped, and burned alive men and women who were not able to flee. The descriptions taken afterwards by the Committee speak eloquently of what took place:

Avakian, Lola, daughter of Pavel, born 1961, living in Sumgait, Quarter 45, Building 10/13, Apartment 37. Attacked in her apartment on 29 February 1988, Lola Avakian was raped and then led nude through the street where she was forced to dance. She was stabbed with a knife, and her body had marks from cigarette burns. She was further mutilated and could only be identified by her little finger. Her father found her body at the Mardakiang morgue. She bore number 71.

Avakian, Yuri, son of Bagrat, living in Sumgait, District 3, Building 5/2, Apartment 47. Cerebral hemorrhage, burns all over the body, slashed with a hatchet and burned at the stake.

Melkoumian. Igor, son of Soghomon. Born 1967, living in Sumgait. Quarter 41A, Building 2B, Apartment 21. Second- and third-degree burns over the entire body, carbon monoxide poisoning, contusions on the neck. After being beaten, he was burned alive in the street. He was killed at the same time as his father, mother, brother, and sister.

Grigorian, Emma, daughter of Chirin, born 1930, living in Sumgait. District 3, Building 5/2, Apartment 45. Stripped and raped. She had a metal pipe shoved into her vagina. Her head was crushed and her ribs broken. Shock, hemorrhage, rupture of the upper vaginal wall, rectal lesions, peritoneal hematoma, rib fractures.

At least seven factors led the Armenians to conclude that Azerbaijani Communist authorities were implicated in these murders.

1. During the days preceding 27 February, the Third Party Secretary of Baku personally participated in several violently anti-Armenian television broadcasts.

2. Some Azerbaijanis in Sumgait, knowing the massacres were coming three days before the 27th, warned some Armenians of their fate.

3. Piles of rocks were delivered beforehand by trucks to the outskirts of the Armenian quarters.

4. The killers were brought to Sumgait in special coaches and vans.

5. Telephone lines linking Sumgait and the outside world were cut before the killings.

6. On 27 February at 9 p.m., Vice-Prosecutor Kadousev appeared on Radio Azerbaijan and gave a false account of the killing of two Azerbaijanis by Armenians. This news was the signal for the violence to begin.

7. Soviet soldiers stood aside for three days, doing nothing to put a stop to the massacres.

The official count lists only thirty-two dead for these three days. During the entire year of 1988, no court was convened to establish the facts or to punish those responsible.

In Soviet Armenia as much as in the diaspora, the slaughter immediately rekindled memories of the genocide and "the dreaded Turk." The authorities openly played on this theme to let the Armenians know they had gone too far and thereby endangered their "hostages" living in areas controlled by the Azerbaijanis.

These massacres sparked a massive immigration of Armenians living in Azerbaijan to the Republic of Armenia, beginning with the survivors of Sumgait. The Karabagh Committee coordinated assistance from the people of the republic to the victims. This solidarity contributed to strengthening the national consciousness of the Armenians.

The Sumgait tragedy strained relations between the Armenians and the Russians. By the terms of the informal pact between the Armenians and the Russians, in effect since 1920, the Armenians accepted Russian tutelage in return for protection from the Turks and Azerbaijanis. This pact had now been broken. From this point on, it was difficult to imagine Mr. Gorbachev as a leader willing to defend the Armenians.

Even more serious was the fact that people convinced of involvement by Azerbaijani Communist authorities in the massacres would naturally ask themselves about the possibility of involvement by the central government. This doubt would inevitably bear on Armenian relations with the Soviet regime.

In memory of the Sumgait victims, 8 March, the day of the annual Soviet "Women's Day," was declared a day of mourning.

On 9 March a meeting in Moscow brought together Mr. Gorbachev, four members of the Politburo, and the First Secretaries of the Armenian and Azerbaijani Communist Parties. They took a Marxist approach to the problem, stripping all national dimensions from the demand for the reunification of Mountainous Karabagh. They recommended measures in the "social, economic, and cultural spheres," and especially a strengthening of "internationalist education."

During these months, the Institute for Oriental Studies in Moscow, charged by the Party to study the Karabagh Question, seized "upon the most minor of incidents to place blame on the Armenians" in order to justify a crackdown in Armenia.

On 21 March *Pravda* published an article admitting that the administration of Mountainous Karabagh had up till then been deficient. The article focused on Boris Kevorkov, the former First Secretary of Mountainous Karabagh, as a scapegoat while at the same time attacking "nationalist demonstrations."

On 22 March at least 100,000 people came together in Yerevan to demonstrate their unhappiness concerning the tendentious presentation of their demands in the national press.

On 23 March the Supreme Soviet rejected an official demand for reunification formulated by the Regional Committee of the Party of Mountainous Karabagh.

In the days preceding the answer announced by Mr. Gorbachev, the authorities arrested the militant nationalist independence advocate Payruir Airikyan, and the army laid siege to the Armenian capital.

On 25 March Mr. Gorbachev announced a *nyet* without concessions to Armenian national demands, leaving Mountainous Karabagh within Azerbaijan. The Secretary General made only a few symbolic gestures, such as the retransmission of television from the Republic of Armenia to Karabagh. The Republic of Azerbaijan would be in charge of the economic credits for the development of Mountainous Karabagh.

Finally, Mr. Gorbachev forbade the demonstration scheduled for 26 March in Yerevan.

26 MARCH TO 7 DECEMBER 1988: FROM NATIONAL ASPIRATIONS TO NATURAL DISASTER

The Armenian national movement slipped out of the regime's hands and developed its own dynamic during this second period. The movement broke with the regime in successive steps: a radicalization of national aspirations (26 March), development of anti-Russian sentiments (5 July), anti-Gorbachevism (18 July), the development of democratic organizations (19 August), the utopian dream of independence (9 September), and a system of dual power coming to the fore (7 November).

Scorned, the Party augmented its repressive apparatus after 7 November, declaring a state of emergency on 24 November, thirteen days before the disaster.

Confronted with Gorbachev's negative response, Armenians decided to demonstrate their disagreement with a one-day "dead city" protest on 26 March. When we ask ourselves what was behind this protest, it is clear that the General Secretary's *nyet* radicalized the Armenian national movement. It served to integrate more political demands, such as the release of Payruir Airikyan, with the search for those truly responsible for the massacres at Sumgait.

The Karabagh Committee and other groups undertook investigations with the refugees to establish the actual toll, substituting themselves in this way for the police authorities.

On 29 March the Armenians were appalled by a television broadcast that attributed the violence equally to the Armenians and Azerbaijanis.

On 30 March a resolution demanding a solution to the Armenian problem was adopted by the Communist Party Committee of Stepanagert, where a general strike paralyzed the city until 8 April.

For 24 April, the commemoration day of the genocide, the authorities closed Armenia to foreigners, fearing a probable explosion. On this day 500,000 people marched peacefully. For the occasion, students placed a cross of stones on the side of the genocide commemoration monument in memory of the victims of Sumgait. People began to equate the Turkish and Soviet threats, linking the date of the genocide, 1915, with the dates of Soviet repression: 1920, 1937, 1949, 1988.

The Armenians still hoped, however, that the XIXth Party Congress on 28 and 29 June would bring them some kind of positive response.

In mid-May the First Party Secretaries of Armenia and Azerbaijan, Demirchian and Bagirov, were dismissed by Moscow and replaced by Haratunian and Vezirov. The joint dismissal of the First Secretaries of Armenia and Azerbaijan irritated the Armenians because it implied that both shared equal responsibility for the violence.

During this same period, 100,000 Armenians demonstrated in Yerevan, demanding punishment for the Sumgait massacres.

The 28th of May, the date of the Republic of Armenia's declaration of independence in 1918, was celebrated for the first time since Sovietization. The appearance of 5,000 demonstrators carrying the tricolor flag of the Republic in the heart of a gathering of tens of thousands and insisting that this day be henceforth a public holiday, marked a radicalization of national aspirations. In addition, General Antranig,* symbol of anti-Turkish struggles, replaced Mr. Gorbachev in the collective imagination.

On 10 June *Pravda* acknowledged for the first time that the authorities had lost control of the situation in Mountainous Karabagh.

On 15 June the Armenian Supreme Soviet opposed the central government by declaring itself unanimously in favor of the reunification of Karabagh. On 17 June the Supreme Soviet of Azerbaijan refused a transfer.

On 28 and 29 June, the Armenians' expectations of change from the XIXth Party Congress were disappointed when the Congress refused to make any concessions. This point-blank refusal triggered off a new round of general strikes.

Meetings resumed in Yerevan at the Opera Square, now rebaptized as "Independence Place" or "Liberty Place," as the case may be.

---

* *Translator's note:* General Antranig (Ozanian, born in 1865) was a legendary Armenian military commander who defended Armenian communities in northeastern Anatolia and the Transcaucasians from 1895 to 1919. He died in Fresno, California, in 1927.

On 5 July the Soviet Army opened fire on demonstrators, killing one and wounding about fifty while dispersing a peaceful demonstration at the Zvartnots Airport in Yerevan.

The first victim of the forces of law and order pushed the movement to a new plane, feeding anti-Russian sentiments. In a parallel development, the official press, continuing its campaign of denigrating Armenians, accused the Armenians of endangering perestroika and promoting "anti-Russian" sentiments, particularly among the Russian intelligentsia.

On 7 July, thousands of people attended the funeral of the demonstrator.

On 12 July the deputies of the Autonomous Region of Mountainous Karabagh voted unilaterally in favor of the reunification of their region with the Republic of Armenia, a clear act of defiance vis-à-vis the central government. On 13 July a spokesman for the Ministry of Foreign Affairs declared that the Party considered the vote null and void.

Fearing an explosion, the central government closed Armenia to visitors from mid-July to mid-August.

On 18 July the televised session of the Supreme Soviet devoted to nationalities shattered all illusions. Gorbachev was revealed as hard and arrogant as he cut off Armenian delegates and refused all concessions. This day represented a new low in Armenian relations with the central government and a virulent "anti-Gorbachevism" was added to already growing "anti-Russian" sentiments.

On 19 July the Attorney General of the U.S.S.R. threatened a curfew if disorders resulted from the denial of the reunification of Mountainous Karabagh with Armenia.

On 20 July hundreds of thousands of Armenians gathered to protest in Yerevan.

On 21 July the militant nationalist Payruir Airikyan was expelled from the Soviet Union.

In August the central government named a mediator, a Russian named Volski, for Karabagh. This appointment pleased neither the Armenians nor the Azerbaijanis.

On 19 August the Armenian nationalist movement went forward by endorsing a program. By means of this program (which appears in its entirety in the appendix), the Committee moved past the issue of territorial demands to lay claim to a liberal-democratic political system that is presented as the only system capable of liberating individual and national talents at the same time that it defends national rights. The signatories have made a break with Marxism, which does not recognize natural rights: the defense of life, individual liberty, and the pursuit of happiness. On the other hand, the Committee does not go so far as to declare itself in favor of independence for Armenia.

By the time this text was conceived, the Karabagh Committee had centered itself around eleven people, most of them affiliated with the universities. None of them had any connection to the local "mafias"—they were honest, and they were recognized by the people as their legitimate representatives.

A succinct biography of each of them follows:

Levon Ter Petrossian, born in 1945, historian with an international reputation, specialist in medieval Armenian literature and the Syriac language.

Alexane Hakobian, born in 1955, historian, specialist in medieval Armenia and the history of modern Karabagh.

Babken Ararktsian, born in 1944, director of conferences at Yerevan State University and chairman of applied mathematics.

Vano Siradeghian, born in 1946, journalist and writer, graduate of the philology program at Yerevan State University, journalism section.

Vazguen Manoukian, born in 1946, professor in the department of applied mathematics at Yerevan State University.

Raphael Ghazarian, born in 1924, professor, head of the department of physics at the Academy of Sciences in Armenia, corresponding member of the Academy of Sciences of the Armenian S.S.R.

Hambardzoum Galoustian, born in 1956, historian, deputy director of the Armenian Ethnographic Museum until he was dismissed during the Karabagh struggles.

Davit Vardanian, born 1950, professor, director of the department of biology, Yerevan State University.

Achot Manoutcharian, born in 1954, assistant principal of School 183 in Yerevan.

Samson Ghazarian, born in 1953, professor of history at School 183 in Yerevan.

Samuel Guevorguian, born in 1949, radio/television commentator in Yerevan.

When the Committee program was published, what was the Armenian frame of mind? A report by Michael Rechtouni, written at the end of the summer and published in the November 1988 issue of *Esprit*, sheds some light on this question. The author notes that among the Armenians one finds "a collective passion and pride in their movement that they themselves did not feel they were capable of."

During Rechtouni's stay in Yerevan, regular meetings on Friday evenings brought the people together. These meetings filled several functions at the same time, including an information function to verify rumors as true or false, an expressive function to allow Committee members to refute point by point the arguments of the central government, and an appropriation function whereby the movement made a claim to the use of public space.

Each family sent at least one member as a representative to participate in the meetings in the former Opera Square. Rechtouni was impressed by the attentiveness of the people present. They did not bother the speakers in case of disagreement and only applauded at the end of each speech. The Armenians were doing their apprenticeship in democracy and liberty.

At this moment Michael Rechtouni observed that:

> The disappointment was strong. The people had been unanimous; their solidarity, their ability to demonstrate peacefully had been rewarded only by a denial that had hurt them deeply. This refusal was, in effect, a bonus for those who had chosen to carry out a pogrom over those who had demonstrated peacefully.

For some, this disappointment led to a decision to emigrate. Rechtouni noted the deeply-rooted desire for independence and concluded that:

the diasporan Armenians are more paralyzed by the situation than those in the Soviet Union. Whereas the latter are no longer imprisoned by the yoke of Soviet culture, the former fear for them. Caught offguard, they realized that their relations with Soviet Armenia were changing drastically. Those who wished to assist the movement often had the impression of being accused by Western public opinion of creating problems for Gorbachev.

Along with ongoing demonstrations in Yerevan, Armenians in the Republic of Armenia developed their relations with Mountainous Karabagh over the summer by means of short visits and economic exchanges.

By the end of August, clashes in Karabagh gave new impetus to the movement. On 2 September demonstrations resumed with greater intensity than before. On 9 September, the movement took a major step when 150,000 to 200,000 Armenians demanded independence while displaying their national flag. On 18 September, there was new violence in Mountainous Karabagh: an Armenian was killed and dozens wounded by Azerbaijanis.

On 19 September tensions mounted in Yerevan, where there was a general strike. Once again the Karabagh Committee asked the Soviet leadership to reconsider its denial of 18 July.

On 21 September exceptional measures were taken, including a curfew imposed on the region of Mountainous Karabagh. During the night of the 21st and 22nd troop reinforcements were sent to Yerevan, with armored vehicles taking positions around government buildings.

On the 30th, the general strike in Yerevan was broken off, but 15,000 police and soldiers remained in place. Stepanagert, the capital of Mountainous Karabagh, remained on strike until 17 October.

Early in October 1988, three Armenian diasporan political parties made a common declaration that called for the Armenian National Movement to halt its strike. It also condemned all extremist actions. This declaration outraged Committee supporters.

On 13 October a member of the Committee, Achot Manoutcharian, and a confidant of the Committee, Khatchik Stamboultsian, were elected deputies to the Supreme Soviet of Armenia.

On 7 November the National Movement took a new step forward. On the occasion of the commemoration of the 1917 Revolution, at the former "Opera Square," nearly one million Armenians taunted party leaders, displayed the Armenian national flag, and demonstrated solidarity with the Committee.

According to Anahide Ter Minassian, while the legitimacy of the Communist authorities was increasingly contested, the Committee was emerging in plain view as the real power and the only representative of a movement whose nature was "revolutionary." It was only when the members of the Committee repeatedly called for withdrawal that their sympathizers left the square. This day proved the existence of a system of dual power, or at least of "alternative" power, in Soviet Armenia.

Seeing its monopoly on power threatened, the Communist Party augmented its pressure. After the Supreme Soviet of Armenia voted on 22 November to recognize each 24 April as a day of commemoration of the genocide, the central government used the pretext of an anti-Armenian pogrom in Kirovabad to declare a state of emergency in Yerevan on 24 November. At the same time it suspended debate in the Armenian Supreme Soviet on the new nationalities law presented by Gorbachev. The Democratic Union saw this as "a military coup d'état," exposing "a rapid movement backward in order to balance political life" in the Soviet Union.[3]

On 25 November, while troops and armor were being deployed in the Caucasus and thousands of Armenians from Azerbaijan (and Azerbaijanis from Armenia) were fleeing, Mr. Gorbachev announced the convocation in Moscow of the official representatives of these two communities.

On 26 November the Soviet army daily *Kraznaia Zvezda* published an alarmist article on the situation in Armenia.[4]

On 28 November, the authorities arrested Sergei Grigoryants, editor-in-chief of the independent journal *Glasnost*, who had gone to Yerevan to investigate. He was sentenced to thirty days in prison.

On 29 November Mr. Gorbachev ordered the official Armenian and Azerbaijani representatives to "eliminate the tension" and "reinforce order and discipline."

In *Le Monde*, put on sale on 5 December (forty-eight hours before the earthquake), Bernard Guetta wrote, "The Soviet leadership finds the hard-line position increasingly tempting." [5] He especially noted a "resolution" of 22 November from the Soviet government, published on 3 December, aimed at making demonstrations illegal and putting the Ministry of Interior and the Prosecutor General of the Ministry of Justice of the Soviet Union in charge of taking action against all violations.

At the same time, the newspaper correspondent added, the central government organized the defense of strategic points: "airports, train stations, oil fields, and communication lines."

NOTES

1. On this subject see *The Republic of Armenia, 1918–1920* by Anahide Ter Minassian. Brussels: Complexe, 1989 (in French).

2. For more information see the article by Alexander Benigsen, "The Caucasian Fuse'" in the journal *Arabies*, nos. 19–20 (July/August 1988) (in French).

3. In "The Declaration of the Democratic Union on Repression in the USSR" published on 25 January 1989 in the newspaper *Gamk*.

4. *Le Monde*, dated 27 November 1988.

5. Dated 6 December 1988.

CHAPTER 6

The Political Earthquake

After the events of 7 December, the Karabagh Committee immediately came to the aid of the disaster victims. But would the government allow the Committee to pursue its humanitarian work without interference? Secretary General Gorbachev arrived in Yerevan on 10 December. Gorbachev did not go to the earthquake zones but spent the day in meetings in the capital.[1]

TAKING BACK THE POLITICAL INITIATIVE

Gorbachev ordered the arrest of Karabagh Committee members and activists. On 10 December at 6:20 p.m., seven of the eleven Committee members were arrested by the army at the Writers' Union building where they had been planning relief efforts. Those arrested were Achot Manoutcharian, Samuel Guevorguian, Babken Ararktsian, Samson Ghazarian, Alexane Hakobian, Vazguen Manoukian, and Levon Ter Petrossian. They were sentenced to thirty days in prison, with the exception of A. Manoutcharian who was a parliamentary deputy. On 13 December another Committee member, Vano Siradeghian, was arrested and on the 14th a close sympathizer of the Committee, parliamentary deputy Khatchik Stamboultsian, was imprisoned.

On 7 January 1989, the authorities arrested four Committee members who had gone underground: Achot Manoutcharian, Raphael Ghazarian, Hambardzoum Galoustian, and Davit Vardanian. By this time, according to the Democratic Union, "nearly 300 Committee activists were in the same position as their leaders." [2]

The authorities "justified" these arrests by claiming that the Committee exploited the situation created by the earthquake to promote their political demands. The witnesses all refuted this assertion. To the contrary, they established that the Committee had set aside its political program as soon as they learned of the disaster in order to aid the survivors.

Nevertheless, on 11 December, Gorbachev, with clenched fists, exclaimed, "Enough!" He labeled the Committee members "political adventurers, both corrupt and dishonest," and he demanded that they cease their activities. [3]

According to A. Manoutcharian, "A new, hysterical propaganda campaign was set loose against the Karabagh Committee." [4] On 16 December *Pravda* published an indictment of the Committee, labeling it "an insult to reason and honor." On 28 December the newspaper *Kommunist* accused Manoutcharian of "preparing armed intervention to obtain Mountainous Karabagh."

The Committee members were sentenced to thirty days in prison and detained there. All were charged in accordance with Article 206.3 of the Soviet Penal Code, which provides for up to three years in prison for "organizing group actions contrary to public order."

The Committee members were all freed on 31 May 1989 without having been put on trial. [5] Without admitting it, the government recognized that the charges were without foundation, although it let the threat of a trial hang over the accused for months.

The second step in retaking control consisted of a shake-up of local authorities. Probably wishing to discipline the military commander in Yerevan for not stopping the Committee members during the initial relief response, Gorbachev replaced him on 10 December with General Makachevitch. [6] He, in turn, ordered the arrest of the Committee members at the end of that same day.

Meanwhile, Minister Ryjkov was displeased on several occasions with the Armenian authorities and their lack of organization during the crisis—"demobilized and incapable of taking any initiative whatsoever."[7] One would think that this would have provided the pretext for dismissing some of those responsible who had been in his line of sight for several months.

What was the role of the military during this process of reasserting authority? Some members of the military were helpful as individuals to survivors. Conscripts were sent to the Yerevan airport to help unload planes bringing foreign humanitarian aid. However, as a military force, the army did not participate in aiding survivors or in removing buried bodies.

During the entire period under consideration—7 December 1988 to 7 January 1989—the state of emergency and the curfew remained in force, with both of them put into place and enforced by the army in Leninakan, Spitak, and the capital.[8] Tanks, the symbols of a military presence, were omnipresent in the region during the entire month of December 1988. A witness described Leninakan on 11 December as "a city under seige."

In the capital city of Yerevan large troop contingents prohibited all gatherings.[9] On 11 December they wounded several people while forcibly dispersing peaceful demonstrators who were protesting the recent arrests of six members of the Committee.[10] One witness, not of Armenian background, felt that the Soviet army was like "an occupying army." Thus the army appeared to be a tool of the central government for disciplining the Committee and the people.

Disaster experts do feel it is necessary to supervise population movements in the affected zones. In the present case, however, the military blockade of the region put into place around 11 December and the pressure to evacuate the population after the 13th took on a political dimension.

After the catastrophe (and contrary to past policy), the authorities issued many visas to Armenians who wanted to emigrate permanently from the Soviet Union. At the time, the people and the foreign relief workers saw this "administrative" policy as an outgrowth of a desire to empty Armenia of its harshest critics in order to regain control over the political situation. In Armenia and in France, the flight of Armenians abroad and to the four corners of the Soviet Union was seen as part of a central government maneuver to break the cohesion of the Armenian nation in the Republic of Armenia.

Did the government crackdown hamper relief efforts? Having to move underground undoubtedly did hamper the activity of the leaders of the Karabagh Committee. Having said so, we must be careful not to exaggerate the damage, because seven members of the Committee were already operating secretly as early as 7 December 1988 in anticipation of the potential arrests of official members.

Yerdjanik Abgarian, Albert Baghdassarian, Avetik Ichkhanian, Archak Sadoyan, Sembat Hakobian, Davit Chahnazarian, and Stepan Karaguebakian had been unofficial participants at Committee meetings for some time. Up till 4 January 1989, four of them coordinated aid with the four remaining members of the Committee who were still underground. Arrested for briefer periods, they pursued the work of the Committee while the official leadership was imprisoned. Slowly they directed the remobilization of the Armenians and were at the head of the demonstrations after 28 February 1989, the anniversary of Sumgait, which marked the emergence of a new political militancy.

There was a great deal of popular anger directed at the government for its failure to provide even a minimum level of organization necessary to facilitate relief efforts. The army, in effect, sealed off the region without any apparent logic, contributing to the creation of terrible traffic problems between the capital and the earthquake zone. Frequently military personnel at numerous roadblocks would lose control of themselves. When they were not firing Kalashnikov rifle volleys into the air, they were smashing headlights on the cars of Armenians who were trying to get to Leninakan to check on the fate of their relatives.

Although members of foreign humanitarian missions were granted dispensations at the start of each day's curfew, there were also numerous refusals and altercations.

PERCEPTIONS OF THE POLITICAL CRACKDOWN

How did members of the Karabagh Committee and the people perceive Gorbachev's policies? Already deeply traumatized by the catastrophe, the people experienced the "political earthquake" as a second disaster. However, they were willing to put their political demands on the back burner in order to give priority to the relief effort. They did not resort to any form of violence as a reaction to the arrests of those whom they regarded as their legitimate representatives.

According to several witnesses, the Armenians, who were in mourning during the month following the earthquake, maintained their dignity and remained determined, mobilized, and committed to their ideals. There was no sign that the disaster or the arrest of the leaders and activists of the Karabagh Committee by the Soviet authorities had broken their democratic aspirations, which had developed during the preceding months.

Several Armenians told witnesses in December that, "For the moment we are setting our political demands aside, but we will take them up again in two months."

After meeting with a group of Armenians in Yerevan, *Le Monde* special correspondent Laurent Grielsammer noted that:

> All of their sympathies were with the Karabagh Committee, which had crystallized the hopes of the Armenian population since February 1988 and had brought together immense crowds to claim the reunification of this territory and to demand the democratization of public life.[11]

Levon Ter Petrossian, a member of the Karabagh Committee, even defended the paradoxical notion that the arrests of the leaders of the national movement sent beneficial shock waves through the community.

The inadequacy of Soviet relief efforts, the ongoing curfew, and the establishment of political control in the context of national mourning only deepened the growing chasm between the Armenians and the Soviet authorities.

International humanitarian relief workers and foreign journalists agreed with them that there were lethal inadequacies in the Soviet government's relief initiative. Several villages, for example, had no outside contact for ten long days. For this reason *Le Monde* did not hesitate to write:

> Thursday, 15 December, a team from the French detachment was the first to reach a large village north of Spitak, only to discover that the inhabitants had all perished—killed not by the earthquake but by the slow pace of relief, absence of needed materials, the short-sightedness of the authorities, and the indifference of the army, which continued to watch the plight of the people with arms crossed. In this single village alone, one hundred and fifty children, isolated and alone, succumbed to injuries, exposure, and gangrene.
>
> Thousands of people who initially survived came to perish in this way, adding a bit more to the common graves.
>
> Must we stress that the authorities forbade foreign relief teams from entering this part of the disaster zone? Must we insist on the fact that the military, ever present, did not want to lend their trucks, which could have made the necessary reconnaissance possible?[12]

Another witness added:

> the continuation of the curfew along with the internment of the Karabagh Committee members and activists who had done their best to organize the first relief response was very badly conceived. A woman expressing a sentiment that was obviously widespread told me, "By arresting the leaders of the Committee who have been giving Gorbachev trouble for a long time, Mr. Gor-

bachev now hopes to dominate a crisis that he was not able to control beforehand."

This official attitude aroused "bitterness and disappointment" among the Armenians according to Raphael Ghazarian, a member of the Committee.[13] At the end of a report filed in early January 1989, Henri de Bresson told his *Le Monde* readers:

> If at the start Mr. Gorbachev represented hopes for the Armenians, the massive presence of Soviet tanks in Yerevan and the dusk-to-dawn curfew have lent legitimacy to the idea that absolutely nothing good could be expected of him.[14]

One witness said that several people had told him:

> Perestroika is a trick thrown out for the consumption of Westerners. Its only merit as far as we're concerned is that it gives us the possibility to talk about our problems. But if they don't resolve them, what good is it to bring them out into the open?

Another witness confirms that:

> Practically no one in Armenia believes in perestroika anymore. From now on Gorbachev has no links vis-à-vis the people. Even the elite barely supports him now.

In December 1988 only 20 percent or less of Amenians supported the government.

Achot Manoutcharian, a Committee member, assessed the reassertion of Moscow's political authority in this way:

> Mr. Gorbachev made an extremely amoral choice. He took advantage of the people's vulnerability after the horrible earthquake to bring down all the force of the repressive apparatus and the propaganda machine on movement activists. Politics founded on lies and amoral-

ity, for which all means are good ones, can only lead to defeat and even tragic consequences.

He added:

> The past seventy years have taught us that if we allow repression, anti-democratic acts, and immorality in one region, however small it may be, this later spreads to other nations and makes its effects felt throughout the world in the form of wars and other catastrophes. There is no need to ask for whom the bell tolls; it tolls for all of us, regardless of the corner of the world in which we live.[15]

In an open letter to the General Secretary, another Committee member, Raphael Ghazarian, declared:

> If you had not delayed and muddled the issue of Mountainous Karabagh, peace and calm would have returned long ago and faith in you and your authority would have gone up all over the world. But unfortunately we are all witnesses to just the opposite. The repression you have launched on such a large scale in Armenia, the arrest of activists, only serves to emphasize the error once more. By stripping the movement of its leadership, you push the people toward actions that are unforeseeable.

Several witnesses shared these concerns and saw Gorbachev's hard-line politics as a "deliberate corruption of the situation."

Ghazarian was equally critical of the Soviet media's role:

> It was clearly immoral and cynical on the part of national television to harp on Azerbaijani aid during the first days of the tragedy, because such aid never existed. There was a flood of telegrams from Azerbaijan into Armenia. These telegrams were full of cruel and perverse joy for Armenia in its moment of sorrow. Trains arriving from Baku had their windows smashed and car-

ried chalk inscriptions, "Our greetings on this happy occasion." On the sixth day three bodies were brought back from Baku, and anti-Armenian pogroms continued in the villages of northern Artsakh (Karabagh).

In a letter addressed to the editor-in-chief of the newspaper *Kommunist*, Ghazarian noted:

> I believe that the fundamental reason for the hasty and provocative confinement of the Committee members and the persecution they endure is that we were on the verge of presenting candidates to serve as people's deputies. The Committee was in a position to prevent the power holders from presenting the people with a final list containing only their candidates as they did before the XIXth Party Congress. If it is really necessary to find someone to accuse of pursuing selfish ends during these sad times for all of our people, it is certainly not the members of the Committee!

At the end of January 1989 three Committee members—A. Manoutcharian, R. Ghazarian, and L. Ter Petrossian—were chosen by the people as candidates for the elections in the month of March, but they could not appear before the people because they were behind bars. When the elections came, the Armenians demonstrated their disaffection through mass absenteeism.

NOTES

1. *Le Monde*, 10, 11, and 14 December 1988.
2. *Gamk*, 25 January 1989.
3. *La Croix*, 13 December 1988.
4. Cf. letter of 18 December published in *Gamk* on 29 December 1988.
5. The Committee members chosen by the candidates in the elections of March 1989 were not able to take part in the general elections.
6. Cf. Achot Manutcharian dated 18 December 1988.
7. *Le Monde*, 20 December 1988.
8. After 12 December, the curfew hours were reduced in Leninakan to midnight to 7 a.m.

9. Fresh troops arrived in Yerevan on 17 December. *Le Monde*, 21 December 1988.

10. *La Croix*, 13 December 1988 and the letter of Achot Manutcharian published in *Gamk* on 29 December 1988.

11. *Le Monde*, 21 December 1988.

12. *Le Monde*, 18 December 1988, article by Laurent Greilsammer.

13. Cf. open letter by R. Ghazarian to Mr. Gorbachev dated 19 December 1988.

14. *Le Monde*, 5 January 1989.

15. Letter of 18 December 1988.

Conclusion

And if there were an earthquake in Yerevan tomorrow?

Several witnesses confided:

After the nightmarish vision of Leninakan, returning to Yerevan was eerie. Built on an earthquake fault similar to Spitak, the Armenian capital has countless buildings with the same shortcomings as those in Leninakan and unable to withstand a major seismic shock. An earthquake is predictable, and if one struck Yerevan tomorrow, where over 1,200,000 people live, there would be more than 100,000 dead.

Without going into details on reconstruction in the earthquake zones, we note that in May 1989 they were still constructing new buildings in Yerevan that were similar to those which collapsed in Leninakan the previous December.

Outside of Armenia, numerous Soviet citizens were outraged by the poor warning system preceding the earthquake and attributed the heavy toll of 7 December 1988 to that fact. Can we expect the creation of a disaster warning system in the Soviet Union within fifteen years?* That would depend on changes in the design and construction of new buildings and on the organization and quality of medical relief.

* *Translator's note:* This question is rendered moot by the December 1991 fall of the Soviet Union. The need persists, but independent Armenia is focused on issues of economic survival and it is doubtful that such a project can emerge as a major national priority in the near future.

Even if there is a true desire for change at the highest levels of Soviet state power, an expert on the limitations of disaster relief:

> strongly doubts that the development of a complete system for disaster warning is possible in the Soviet Union within such a short time frame. It would require radical changes in the political system and the behavior of individuals.

> First of all, the system must admit that no society is free from the threat of disasters. It must then take steps that give priority to the individual insofar as political and economic choices are concerned. It must also develop a response system that resembles ORSEC and SAMU. At their core, these organizations demand that their members possess a high level of expertise, be autonomous, and be capable of quick and sure decisions without looking for ways to sidestep their responsibilities.

FURTHER IMPROVEMENTS IN PRIVATE RELIEF AID

To our knowledge, French governmental aid to Armenia was not criticized. This was not the case for private humanitarian aid. Although such aid comes from a strong sense of generosity, it can backfire if it is not properly administered.

The flood of aid in response to the earthquake of 7 December made clear once again that aid must be adapted to the real needs of the victims, and that there is a responsibility to determine those needs as rapidly and accurately as possible before launching appeals for contributions. Otherwise tons of unusable materials pile up in airport hangars.

To be put to use easily, contributions of clothes, medicines, and materials must be sorted out, in usable condition, and labeled in English and if possible in the language of the country for which it is destined. In order to ensure that these goods are received by those for whom they are destined, the donors must accompany them to their destination.

Experience has also shown that gifts of money to humanitarian organizations are more valuable than gifts of materials, because they allow the purchase of materials that truly fill people's needs. Finally, humanitarian organizations must rigorously control information that they issue to the media in order to avoid the circulation of unfounded rumors.

Epilogue

LEVON CHORBAJIAN

Pierre Verluise ends his account on 7 January 1989. The unprecedented scale of change since that time was unforeseen by nearly everyone, and Gorbachev's pledge to rebuild the earthquake-ravaged zones within two years proved wildly unrealistic. Even if political calm had prevailed, shortcomings in Soviet infrastructure and technology would have made that an impossible deadline to meet. Rather, two years after Gorbachev's pledge, most of the reconstruction remained to be done and the Soviet Union itself was in the grip of an upheaval that left it a scant year to live. At the end of 1991, the Soviet Union was dissolved into a large Russian Federation and fourteen newly independent states, including Armenia.

Due to the worldwide generosity of people and their governments in providing money, materials, and volunteers, there were impressive accomplishments in earthquake reconstruction during this period. Among the noteworthy projects are the construction of the Norwegian hospital, the Italian and Austrian villages, the German homes, and the English, Hungarian, and Mongolian schools. The U.S. government provided earthquake relief and has followed that up with food aid, which has alleviated some of the hardship imposed by Azerbaijani blockades of the 1990s. Armenian organizations in the diaspora have also made important investments in housing, education, agriculture, health care, and food technology.[1]

Accomplishments fell far short of the need, however, and staggering problems remain. By the end of 1992, only 20 percent of the reconstruction had been completed, and Armenia still had over half a million homeless victims of natural and political upheavals. The World Bank allocated $28 million in loans for earthquake reconstruction in 1994. This will allow for the completion of still unfinished apartments and the repair of partially damaged buildings and new construction, including single-family owner-occupied homes, water and sewage projects, and workplace investments. The loan, however, does not address what has been the major stumbling block to rebuilding—the shortage of building materials due to the blockade.

Post-traumatic stress disorder remains a serious problem among survivors, with its accompanying symptoms of flashbacks, nightmares, and depression. Adding to the grief is a deep sense of collective loss in a society where individualism was not strongly rooted and where a person's primary loyalties were based on extended family and friendship networks. Armenians drew meaning and definition in life from long-standing, repetitive human contacts, some of which spanned entire lifetimes. When an elderly woman, an earthquake survivor from Spitak, told me, "There is almost no one left," she was referring to the loss of the intensely woven, textured, and irreplaceable patterns of her community life.

For some, these losses were unbearable, and one aftermath of the earthquake was the dramatic increase in suicides in a region where suicide rates were among the world's lowest. For the majority who have survived the earthquake, the fractured social networks are a permanent legacy of their experience and an open wound that can never heal.

Few Western experts foresaw the furious changes that overtook the Soviet Union.[2] Armenia was a leading actor in these events, and the dynamic of change bounded back and bore upon her. Here, with the advantage of hindsight, we can appreciate Pierre Verluise's wisdom in including the struggle over Mountainous Karabagh in his discussion of the earthquake. The involvement of the Karabagh Committee in earthquake relief and the arrest of its members in December/January 1988–1989 overlaid the earthquake with stark political drama.

Since that time, progress in earthquake reconstruction and the fate of the survivors have been defined by much broader events, including the dissolution of the Soviet Union, the Armenian–Azerbaijani conflict over Mountainous Karabagh, and ethnic turmoil in neighboring Georgia. As a result, the Armenian earthquake has become a political earthquake to an even greater degree than described by Verluise.

1989–1993

Demonstrations in Yerevan continued throughout the late winter and early spring of 1989. They were smaller than the massive demonstrations of the year before, but they did reach levels of several hundred thousand participants, and, even though smaller, they were enthusiastic. Raised fists and spirited chants of "*Gomida! Gomida!*" [Committee! Committee!] filled the streets and parks as the crowds expressed their faith in the still imprisoned members of the Karabagh Committee. In late May, the Committee members were released without trial, and later the Karabagh Committee voluntarily disbanded and reconstituted itself as a popular front. As the official opposition to the Armenian Communist Party, the Armenian National Movement (*Hayots Hamazgayn Sharzhum*) assumed broad responsibility for Armenia's future.

In August 1990 Armenia declared itself an independent and sovereign state. In September 1991 Armenians went to the polls to vote on independence. The turnout was over 95 percent of the eligible voters, and 99.3 percent voted in favor of independence. The next month Levon Ter Petrossian, a historian, won a multiparty election and assumed the office of president. Ter Petrossian was an original member of the Karabagh Organizing Committee; only two and a half years earlier he had been a prisoner in Gorbachev's jails along with the other members of the Committee.

The task of the Ter Petrossian government is difficult, as it is in all of the post-Soviet states. The transition to a capitalist economy has created serious problems, including rapid inflation without concomitant wage increases, breakdowns in production, the interruption of trade, and the erosion of the Communist safety net, resulting in unemployment, homelessness, and destitution.[3]

Although all of the former Soviet minority republics (and Russia herself) face daunting problems, Armenia is among the least fortunate in some respects. A few comparisons will make this clear. The former Baltic republics are not under economic blockade, as is Armenia, and they have an outlet to the sea, which gives them access to Finland, Scandinavia, and Germany. There were unresolved questions concerning Russian military forces on Baltic soil, but these troops were withdrawn by the fall of 1994. The matter of unwanted Russian settlers throughout the region remains, but nowhere in the Baltics does this issue come close to matching the violent confrontations gripping the Transcaucasus. The Ukraine possesses some of the world's richest farmland and abundant coal reserves. Georgia, despite open political conflicts and minority secessionist movements, has much arable land and a Black Sea coastline. Although Azerbaijan's oil and natural gas production were long thought to have peaked and her reserves dwindling, recent offshore discoveries and access to Western oil and natural gas extraction technologies promise large future revenues.[4] The Central Asian states, for all of their economic underdevelopment and their regional quarrels, possess vast energy and mineral reserves and are being openly courted by Turkey, Iran, and Pakistan.[5]

By contrast, Armenia seems dwarfed by its problems. Most of the terrain is mountainous or rocky high plain, there is little arable land and few forests, and copper and molybdenum are the only minerals that are easy to exploit commercially. More serious is the fact that Armenia has no indigenous energy sources and no neighbors through which energy can be reliably imported.[6] If Armenia had a border with the Russian Federation, she could import fuel and raw materials and component parts for factories, and export finished goods with relative ease and security. However, Armenia's "impossible geography" denies her such a possibility. Armenia faces a troubled Georgia and a hostile Azerbaijan between herself and Russia.

In the Soviet era, railways and pipelines through Georgia and Azerbaijan linked Armenia with the rest of the Soviet Union, with 85 percent of the goods coming into Armenia through Azerbaijan and 15 percent through Georgia. Faced with intermittent but damaging Azerbaijani supply blockades after the Karabagh protests began, Armenia was able to shift this ratio to 75–25 percent and survive, but only under very poor conditions. During the winter of 1991–1992 schools, universities, and cultural institutions were closed for lack of heat, 10 of Yerevan's 38 hospitals had no heat, half of all apartments were heated only a few hours a day and the rest not at all, and there were major electrical blackouts.[7] Conditions during the winter of 1992–1993 were worse than the year before, and 1993–1994 was little better. As a hospital physician in the earthquake-ravaged city of Leninakan describes it:

> How we lived through this winter is hard to imagine. Of course it is better to see it once than to hear about it many times, but I would not wish those inhuman conditions on my friends or any other human being. The wards of the intensive care unit were like silent and cold caves where the temperature in the night went down to 0° Celsius (32° Farenheit). There was no way to heat the intravenous solutions. Even if we could heat them, they would turn cold again in a few minutes. It makes no sense to speak about monitoring the patients because in the night, under candlelight, it was difficult to see the natural color of a patient's face. People were waiting for morning to come. We had many cases of frostbite and many deaths.[8]

The lack of heat, fuel, raw materials, and component parts have ground the economy to a halt for the third year in a row. Under these conditions—for the most part brought on by the Azerbaijani blockade—there has been scant progress on earthquake reconstruction. Armenia cannot receive building materials from outside of her borders, nor can she manufacture them in her largely idle factories, shut down for lack of raw materials and energy.

Without a Karabagh settlement, the Azerbaijanis will not lift their economic blockade of Armenia, and the resulting stranglehold over the Armenian economy will not be eased. A settlement, however, has proven elusive. Various third parties, among them the Baltic Council, Russian and Kazakh presidents Boris Yeltsin and Nursultan Nazarbayev, and the Iranian government have negotiated cease-fires. Some lasted only a few hours, and until 1994, none held.

Armenia, Azerbaijan, and Karabagh have been toured by former U.S. Secretary of State Cyrus Vance, representing the United Nations, and the Conference on Security and Cooperation in Europe (CSCE)[9] has considered the issue and sent its president, former Czechoslovak Prime Minister Jiri Dienstbier, on a fact-finding mission. Dienstbier was able to bring the Armenians and the Azerbaijanis together for talks in Helsinki in March of 1992. Dialogue continued, but there were no lasting cease-fires or terms of settlement acceptable to all parties. Nor was any outside party willing to commit peacekeeping forces.

In lieu of such a commitment, the region has been gripped by war. For the overwhelming majority of Mountainous Karabagh residents (i.e., the Armenians), Azerbaijani rule—whether exercised by a Soviet republic or an independent state—has little or no legitimacy. Throughout 1991 the Azerbaijani government responded to this situation in the only way it could, given its refusal to surrender its hold on Karabagh, and that was to try to shift the demographic balance by settling Azerbaijanis in Mountainous Karabagh and terrorizing the Armenian residents, forcing them to flee the territory.

This process was documented by a multinational delegation from the First International Andrei Sakharov Memorial Congress that visited Armenia and Azerbaijan in May 1991. The delegation was led by Lady Baroness Caroline Cox of the British House of Lords. The delegation sought and was repeatedly refused permission to visit Mountainous Karabagh by the Azerbaijani government, but it was able to inspect Armenian and Azerbaijani villages in border areas between the two republics. The deportations from the Armenian village of Getushen, in Azerbaijan, were typical of what the observers found:

> During the deportations there were numerous civil rights violations of several types. People were killed sin-

gly and multiply. There were beatings, rapes, forced ab-
ductions, and imprisonment. Property and livestock
were stolen or bought for an insulting price, such as a
car for two roubles. Voluntary requests to leave were
obtained at gun point. Ears of girls were torn by forcible
removal of earrings. We found no evidence, in spite of
diligent inquiry, that anyone recently deported from
Getushen left it voluntarily.

Most of the witnesses told us that the beatings and
killings were carried out by the Azerbaijan OMON (local militia). But the Soviet army organized the surrounding of the villages and taunted the villagers, "Why
have you not left already?" Then they stood aside while
the OMON terrorized the villagers. The villagers were
left on the Armenian side of the border with only the
clothes they were wearing.[10]

While the violence continued on the ground, major political
changes were taking place. Mountainous Karabagh held its own
referendum on independence in December 1991. Independence
was approved nearly unanimously. The government of Azerbaijan denounced the election as illegal. In January 1992 Mountainous Karabagh petitioned the United Nations for recognition
but did not receive it. In fact, recognition has not been extended by any international body or nation, including the Republic of Armenia, which fears that recognition would lead to a
declaration of war by Azerbaijan.

Karabagh's declaration of independence has, however, allowed Armenia to assume a new posture with regard to the
conflict. Armenia no longer seeks the reunification of Mountainous Karabagh with Armenia nor does it have any other territorial claim on Azerbaijan. Armenia insists that the conflict is
now between the people of Mountainous Karabagh, who seek
self-determination, and the Republic of Azerbaijan, which refuses to recognize that right. Armenia now defines herself as an
interested third party but not a direct participant. Despite this
change in Armenian policy, the Azerbaijani economic blockade

continues, and Armenian border areas have been subjected to relentless shelling.

The rebellion in Mountainous Karabagh has had its own profound effect on Azerbaijan. The Azerbaijani reform movement was indelibly marked from the start by the fact that glasnost-style politics in the republic were initiated by the Armenians in Mountainous Karabagh. Furthermore, the issue has been at the forefront of concerns in Azerbaijan since early 1988—at the expense of other issues such as democratization, reform, and substantive economic matters.[11] Thus the pacification of Mountainous Karabagh's rebellious Armenians became the litmus test for political success in the republic, and as resistance has grown, repression has followed in an ever escalating and destructive cycle. The Azerbaijani Communist Party's ability to manipulate the Karabagh question accounted for its hold on power long after the Communists had been replaced in other republics.[12]

Mountainous Karabagh's declaration of independence was a clear indication of its willingness and ability to defy Baku. As the Azerbaijani government's weakness became increasingly clear, its hold on power became increasingly tenuous in the face of growing opposition by the Azerbaijani Popular Front. The Azerbaijani government's response was to shore up its deteriorating political position by escalating the violence in the search for a military solution. Helicopter gunships and GRAD rocket launchers that fire forty shells at a time were deployed. Relentless Azerbaijani bombardment had reduced Stepanagert, Karabagh's capital of 60,000 inhabitants, to rubble by the spring of 1992. The *Christian Science Monitor* reported that:

> The population lives much of the day underground in cold basement cellars. A warren of rooms under one apartment is reserved for women and children who sleep there three or four to a bed. The men lie in the corridors.[13]

Baroness Cox who visited Mountainous Karabagh on numerous occasions during 1991 and 1992 added these poignant details:

to compound the agony of the people caught in this besieged, bombarded city, the blockade has prevented the delivery of medical supplies . . . surgeons are operating with no anesthetics or analgesics, relying on vodka to provide some pathetically inadequate sedation for major trauma, including amputations and burns. The blockade also prevents the evacuation of the injured to hospitals in Armenia. The hospital and the maternity hospital have been further damaged by shelling; mothers are giving birth in improvised wards in the basement of the Town Hall, but this has since been destroyed by shells; the fate of the mothers underneath is not known. The death rate among babies is increasing; many are born prematurely; many mothers do not have milk; and there are no supplies of baby formula.[14]

Despite these assaults, Mountainous Karabagh's Armenians were able to take advantage of political confusion in Azerbaijan to launch successful offensives against Azerbaijani forces in early 1992. By June, Azerbaijani units had been defeated and were forced to withdraw from all of Mountainous Karabagh, including the fortress city of Shushi, the only sizable settlement with an Azerbaijani majority. It had not been in Armenian hands since 1920.

In early March 1992, Armenian forces in Mountainous Karabagh were accused of massacring 1,000 Azerbaijanis, largely civilians in the village of Khodjalu.[15] The Armenians denied any massacre and said they were forced to take the village because it was being used as a base for the bombardment of Stepanagert. There were conflicting reports from non-Armenian sources that called the Azerbaijani allegations into question.[16]

The publicity given to the Khodjalu allegations in Azerbaijan, combined with Azerbaijani military reversals throughout the spring of 1992, caused widespread discontent with the government of Ayaz Mutalibov. He was replaced by Yakub Mamedov, who was discredited by the fall of Shushi and the loss of the Lachin Strip, a narrow strategic band of land that separated Armenia from Mountainous Karabagh and whose capture gave Armenia direct land access to Karabagh.[17] In the wake of these defeats, Mamedov fell in the 7 June Azerbaijani presidential elections to Abulfaz Elchibey, head of the Azerbaijani Popular Front.

Elchibey openly allied himself with Turkey and soon launched Azerbaijani offensives as part of his pledge to retake Mountainous Karabagh within two months.[18] The Azerbaijanis quickly took the Shahumian district, an Armenian-populated area directly to the north of Mountainous Karabagh. By the end of the summer, Azerbaijani forces had retaken one-fourth of Mountainous Karabagh and one-half by the end of 1992. Armenians in these areas were either killed or had fled.

Elchibey appeared to bring Azerbaijan the political stability it had lacked. However, while the Azerbaijanis achieved military successes under Elchibey, these fell far short of Elchibey's promises and came at a high cost in casualties. Beginning in early 1993, Karabagh Armenian forces launched new counteroffensives and achieved rapid military victories. A second corridor was opened between Armenia and Mountainous Karabagh with the taking of Kelbajar in the spring. Mountainous Karabagh was retaken from the Azerbaijanis by late June, and over the summer Armenian forces moved east to take the city of Aghdam, which served as the key base for Azerbaijani military operations in Mountainous Karabagh. Armenian forces also threatened the Azerbaijani town of Fizuli to the south of Mountainous Karabagh.

These reversals precipitated a new Azerbaijani political crisis. An armed mutiny led by Col. Surat Husseinov, a former Azerbaijani military commander in Mountainous Karabagh, moved on Baku and forced President Elchibey to flee the city. Parliament stripped Elchibey of his office in late June. Husseinov was made prime minister and the office of president went to Gaidar Aliyev.

Aliyev had most recently been the head of the Azerbaijani province of Nakhichevan, but his past positions are the more revealing ones. Aliyev was the head of the Azerbaijani Communist Party, a top KGB official, and a Brezhnev appointee to the Soviet Politburo where he served until removed by Gorbachev in 1987. Aliyev's remarkable comeback seemed to signal a repudiation of at least the public aspects of Elchibey's pro-Turkish policies and a turn to Russia, but what this meant for Armenia and the conflict over Mountainous Karabagh was unclear.

In Armenia, the Ter Petrossian government desperately wants peace so it can begin the staggering task of rebuilding its shattered economy, a task that includes a full 80 percent of the earthquake reconstruction. Ter Petrossian's repudiation of union with Mountainous Karabagh is designed to achieve this objective, but three factors render it elusive.

First are the Karabagh Armenians themselves, who have put nearly seventy-five years of Azerbaijani rule behind them and feel they can never return to the *status quo ante*.

Second, Ter Petrossian faces opposition in Armenia from those who reject his moderate Karabagh policy as a betrayal. In June 1992 there was a demonstration of 100,000 in Yerevan called by the National Front, a coalition of opposition political parties in Parliament. August brought smaller demonstrations of 50,00, which called for Ter Petrossian's resignation and a failed no-confidence debate in Parliament. These demonstrations have continued into 1993 and 1994 with the National Democratic Union emerging as a major opposition group. By now several members of the Karabagh Organizing Committee—Achot Manoutcharian, Davit Vardanian, and Vazguen Manoukian—had joined the opposition. Manoutcharian, Ter Petrossian's former national security adviser, has been particularly outspoken in making allegations of governmental corruption and serious human rights violations by the Ministry of the Interior. At the end of three years of economic hardship and the continuing war over Karabagh, Ter Petrossian's popular support has declined. The government remains stable, but challenged, and it does not control the independence-minded Karabagh Armenians. Ter Petrossian has pledged to come directly to Karabagh's defense if the territory were ever in danger of being overrun and its people subject to slaughter, but there are many who would like him to be doing more now. In such circumstances, he would certainly face a serious backlash in light of a settlement that was seen as a sellout.

The third factor is Azerbaijan. No major Azerbaijani political figure has been willing to concede Karabagh, and Aliyev, like his predecessor, has pursued a military victory. He has not been so pro-Russian and anti-Turkish as some expected, but has pursued a pragmatic policy of seeking diplomatic and military aid from numerous sources while making as few concessions on Karabagh and to the Russians as possible. Aliyev publicly appears to be open to the proposal for Karabagh autonomy within Azerbaijan put forth by the Russians and the CSCE in the spring of 1994. "Autonomy," however, has yet to be defined, and it is safe to say that Aliyev's version will fall short of the expectations of the Karabagh Armenians.

Iran, Turkey, the United States, and Russia are all interested parties to the conflict, in part because of the potential for a wider regional war.[19] Each has its own agenda, but Russia, because of its geographical proximity and its greater political and military muscle in the region, emerged in 1993 as the major outside player.

Iran and Turkey are competitors for influence in the region. Iran shares borders with both Armenia and Azerbaijan. Iran also has a large Azerbaijani minority in the northwest where the Iranian–Azerbaijani border is located. The Azerbaijanis in Iran have shown no disloyalty to Iran, but there are militants to the north who view these Iranian Azerbaijanis as a captive minority. Elchibey's pro-Turkish policies were threatening to Iran because they could have served as the basis for an ambitious pan-Turkic irredentism that would have encompassed northwestern Iran.

Elchibey later muted his anti-Iranian rhetoric. Aliyev's policies have been more even-handed throughout the region, seeking aid wherever the promise of it exists. Though he fears Russian influence and he rejects Russian troops and an exclusively Russian peacekeeping force in a Karabagh settlement, Aliyev's policies are more Moscow- than Ankara-centered, and this has stabilized Azerbaijani–Iranian relations.

Iran has strongly condemned the success of the Armenians in expanding out of Karabagh into Azerbaijan proper and to the Azerbaijan–Iran border. At the same time they have kept the lines of communication open with Azerbaijan and Armenia, and they continue to trade with Armenia. Overall, Iran's policy has been reactive rather than proactive and geared to protecting its own territorial and political integrity.

Turkey publicly calls for the integrity of existing borders (i.e.

Azerbaijan keeps Mountainous Karabagh) but covertly seeks ful-
fillment of its longstanding objective of direct territorial linkage
between Turkey and Azerbaijan, and, via the Caspian Sea, to
Central Asia, where four of the five former Soviet republics have
Turkic majorities.[20] Standing in the way of this ambition are
Armenia's southern provinces and her narrow border with Iran.

What would be ideal for Turkey and Azerbaijan is to draw
Armenia into a brief but intense war between Armenia and
Azerbaijan, with Turkey aiding the Azerbaijanis but putting up a
publicly neutral face. Armenia would be subdued and forced to
surrender her southern provinces, thus linking the two Turkish
states to the east (Azerbaijan) and west (Turkey) of Armenia.
The shelling of Armenia by Azerbaijan and the blockade are
designed as the provocation for such a war, but Armenia, so far
mindful of the consequences, has not taken the bait.

Turkey's agenda faces two major constraints. First is Turkey's
desire to be admitted to the European Economic Community.
Turkish overtures have brought her human rights record under
scrutiny. Most of the attention has focused on the denial of
human rights to Turkey's large Kurdish minority and the treatment of dissident students, workers, and others who have opposed Turkish state policies. Direct Turkish intervention on behalf of Azerbaijan would be politically damaging to Turkey's
European ambitions in its own right, and it would draw unwanted attention to these other issues. The issue of the Armenian genocide has already been raised in the European Parliament. Turkish involvement, therefore, has been either unofficial
or as carefully concealed as possible with the intent that Azerbaijan should appear to be acting on its own.

The second constraint is the Russian Federation. Turkey has
increased its troop concentrations along the entire Turkish–Armenian border, bringing its forces face to face with Russian
forces in Armenia. Following Armenian victories in Shushi and
the Lachin Strip in May 1992, Turkish Foreign Minister Hikmet
Cetin warned Armenia that "Turkey will never allow a change
by force in the legal facts of Nagorno–Karabagh. Armenia will
be responsible for the grave consequences that arise from such
an action." Turkey backed off from this threat after the Military
Chief of the Commonwealth States, Marshal Yevgeni Shaposh-

nikov, warned that any Turkish intervention could spark a third world war.[21]

The Turkish Defense Minister, Nevzat Ayaz, has denied the participation of any Turkish troops in the Karabagh conflict, although he did acknowledge that retired Turkish generals may have gone to Azerbaijan on their own initiative. At least one Turkish and one Arabic paper report more direct involvement. A story in the 5 July 1992 issue of *Cumhuriet* (a Turkish paper) reported that ten Turkish generals were in Azerbaijan to train military forces there. On 10 July *Alshark-el-Aswat* (an Arabic paper) reported the presence of over 1,000 Turkish military specialists, including 160 officers, in Azerbaijan. Alpaslan Turkesh, founder of the Turkish fascist Gray Wolves, admitted that his followers were fighting in Karabagh with Azerbaijani forces.[22] Since that time President Aliyev has imported as many as 2,000 *mujaheddin* fighters from Afghanistan as well as other mercenary forces.

The Bush administration's emphasis on foreign policy did not extend to Transcaucasia, and with the Clinton administration the focus has shifted from foreign to domestic issues such as unemployment, national health insurance, and the federal deficit. Yet we can discern several continuities in U.S. policy and actions, despite the transition in administrations. First, the United States has joined other Western industrial nations in shipping food and other humanitarian aid to Armenia during the winters of the 1990s. In what have been repeatedly described as near famine conditions, these contributions have helped to avert catastrophe.

Second, the United States continues to defer to Turkey as the vehicle for extending Western influence into the former Soviet republics, in particular in the regions of Transcaucasia and Central Asia. The United States is concerned about the spread of Islamic fundamentalism associated with Iran. For this reason and as an extension of its longstanding political and military ties to Turkey, the United States sees Turkey as an appropriate model, i.e., "a democratic secular state" with a "free market economy," for post-Soviet development in these new nations.

The United States has joined other non-combatant powers in insisting on the integrity of existing borders (Azerbaijan keeps

Karabagh), and has been openly critical of Karabagh Armenian offensives in the Lachin Strip, Kelbajar, and other areas. At the same time, the United States has been much less outspoken about the Azerbaijani blockade of Armenia and remained silent on Azerbaijan's shelling of Mountainous Karabagh and Armenia. This U.S. double standard mirrors the American–Turkish alliance. It is also a reflection of the fact that the largest U.S. commercial interests in the region lie with Azerbaijani oil and natural gas deposits. U.S. policy seeks a solution that would allow for safe corporate investment in Azerbaijan and the construction of the most direct and least expensive Azerbaijani–Turkish pipeline, which would have to go through Armenia. Continued armed conflict and a larger regional war are not in the interests of the United States—and certainly not with the Karabagh Armenians on the offensive—and hence the United States joined in the international peace initiatives of 1993.

U.S. policy, however, has been more even-handed than its Turkish connection might indicate. There has been some pressure from the United States on Turkey, not always effective, to allow humanitarian aid to pass through Turkey to Armenia. The United States has also imposed a trade embargo on Turkey's ally Azerbaijan in response to the Azerbaijani blockade of Armenia, and efforts by Turkey's supporters in Congress to overturn the embargo have not been successful.

The Russian presence in the southern Transcaucasus predates the Bolshevik Revolution by a century. That presence was deeply compromised by the dissolution of the Soviet Union and the assertion of Armenian, Azerbaijani, and Georgian independence. Furthermore, all three republics have had reason to suspect Russian motives. The Georgians will not soon forget the Soviet massacres of Georgian nationalists in Tbilisi in April 1989, nor the Azerbaijanis the Soviet occupation of Baku in January 1990. The Georgians charge the Russians with support for Abkhazian and Ossetian separatists. And both the governments in Baku and Yerevan feel that the Russians have at various times sided with their protagonists.

Russia's own severe political and economic problems, which in some ways mirror those of the former minority republics, have been an obstacle to broad and direct Russian involvement.

However, the Russian Federation remains, without question, the preemineent regional power, and it was only a matter of time before Russia would begin to reassert its authority in a region it regards as within its sphere of influence. Ethnic conflicts in the Transcaucasus have provided an avenue for renewed Russian involvement in the region, and we began to see this in 1993 with regard to the Karabagh struggle.

There is agreement between the United States and Turkey and at the United Nations that the proper mediator for the conflict should be the Conference for Security and Cooperation in Europe (CSCE), and, in particular, its nine-member Minsk Group, which is charged with negotiating a solution to the conflict. The Minsk Group includes Turkey and Russia. March 1992 meetings held in Helsinki did establish the basis for an ongoing dialogue among the warring parties. An important breakthrough came in 1993 when Azerbaijan set aside its objections to the participation of Mountainous Karabagh on the basis that Karabagh's direct involvement would convey recognition of Karabagh's status as an entity separate from Azerbaijan. But this development was tempered by the fact that CSCE had no military or peacekeeping forces at its command, and therefore no enforcement power for the settlement of the crisis.[23]

In the wake of Karabagh Armenian victories in the spring of 1993, the international community and CSCE put forth a proposal for negotiations. The Three Plus One Peace initiative drew its name from its three major sponsors, the United States, Turkey, and Russia, along with the CSCE and its Minsk Group. The proposal called for the withdrawal of Karabagh Armenian forces from Kelbajar and a sixty-day cease-fire followed by peace talks.

Azerbaijan, badly battered by Karabagh Armenian offensives, immediately accepted these terms, and the Armenian government followed suit later, but the Karabagh Armenians refused and then demurred because they felt the terms of the proposal failed to take into consideration the security needs of the territory. They had taken Kelbajar specifically because it had been used as a staging area for Azerbaijani offensives, and the proposal was asking them to return it without any guarantee that Azerbaijan would not use it to resume its offensives.

The Three Plus One initiative was a proposal for a cease-fire; it did not even begin to address what a peace settlement would look like. Nevertheless, the continuing dialogue did represent a formal, ongoing search for peace, and it stood as a hopeful sign in an otherwise grim scenario.

1994

That hope was shattered when Aliyev broke a Russian/CSCE-mediated cease-fire and launched a major offensive along the entire eastern Karabagh front on 18 December 1993. After initial Azerbaijani successes in driving the Armenians back, the Azerbaijanis were forced to retreat, and little territory ended up changing hands. However, the Azerbaijanis were attacking entrenched Armenian positions in rugged mountainous terrain, and the casualty rates were frightful. Over 8,000 Azerbaijanis were killed along with 700 Karabagh Armenians and 300 from the Republic of Armenia. We can make these figures more meaningful, perhaps, by extrapolating the battlefield deaths on to an equivalent U.S. population during the Vietnam War era. If we assume that Karabagh, Azerbaijan, and Armenia each have a population equal to the U.S. population during the Vietnam era (220 million), we would have over 1 million deaths for Karabagh (actual population 150,000), 250,000 for Azerbaijan (actual population 7 million), and 19,000 for Armenia (actual population 3.5 million) in a three-month period. This compares with 55,000 U.S. battlefield deaths during the entire course of the Vietnam War.

This deadliest phase of the war had spent itself by mid March. The Russians arranged a cease-fire in early May. This was extended on 27 July, and the cease-fire held through the fall months. The Russian peace proposal contains four major provisions. (1) Karabagh will remain a part of Azerbaijan but with autonomy. (2) There will be a demilitarized zone around the enclave. (3) There will be open lines of access between Armenia and Karabagh via the Lachin Strip and Kelbajar. (4) Russian military forces will guarantee this arrangement on behalf of the United Nations.

The Russian proposal serves as a basis for negotiation, but many issues stand in the way of a final settlement. Among them are:

1. Autonomy is undefined, and in any case we can expect the Karabagh Armenians to be highly skeptical of it. Autonomy was granted to the Karabagh Armenians when the territory was originally ceded to Azerbaijan in the early 1920s, and the people saw that it quickly came to naught.

2. Azerbaijan wants a withdrawal of Karabagh Armenian forces from its occupied territory and a resettlement of its refugees as a precondition for negotiations.

3. Armenia first wants a cease-fire and negotiations to determine the terms of settlement, which will include a withdrawal from Azerbaijani lands.

4. Turkey has volunteered 1,500 troops to help monitor the peace settlement.

5. Armenia and Karabagh reject the presence of any Turkish troops.

6. Russia wants to deploy its troops only to monitor a settlement and seeks to limit the CSCE to contributing to the costs of maintaining a peacekeeping force.

7. Swedish diplomat Jan Eliasson who serves as the chairman of the Minsk Conference on Nagorno–Karabagh wants a multinational CSCE peacekeeping force.

8. The United Nations has rejected a Russian petition to have U.N. peacekeeping status for its military forces, saying that this could only be done if the Russian troops were part of a multinational force under U.N. control.

9. Turkey and Azerbaijan do not want Russian troops to monitor a settlement, and certainly not troops composed only of Russians. To undercut Russian initiatives to monitor a settlement alone, they propose a CSCE force of which Turkey would be a part. In addition,

Azerbaijan proposes that no more than 30 percent of the peacekeeping force come from one country.

10. Finally—and critically—the Karabagh Armenians have so far won the war on the ground, and they have tasted freedom and liked it. It is an open question whether they could be pressured into accepting autonomy within Azerbaijan after putting up such a gallant and successful fight against overwhelming numerical odds.[24]

This political discussion brings us full circle back to the terrible human tragedy of the 1988 earthquake. From the vantage point of 1994, the earthquake appears distant because the natural disaster was soon subsumed within a whirlwind of larger political passions and war. It is only through the resolution of those complex issues that the material and human resources for full earthquake reconstruction will be made available once again.

NOTES

1. The scale and scope of international aid was impressive. Over 100 nations sent assistance, and the total value of aid exceeded $500 million, the largest international response ever to a natural disaster. Tony Halpin, "Disaster and Recovery," *AIM* (January 1991), pp. 20–22.

2. For an exception see Alexander J. Motyl, *Sovietology, Rationality, Nationality: Coming to Grips with Nationalism in the USSR* (New York, 1990).

3. The median 1987 monthly wage of 340 roubles increased to 400 roubles in 1992, but this increase fell far short of covering the dramatic, across-the-board increases in pricing due to shortages, cutbacks in government subsidies, and the introduction of capitalist pricing mechanisms. We can see this by comparing 1987 to 1992 prices for selected commodities:

Commodity	1987 price	1992 price
kg. of chicken	3.5 roubles	45 roubles
30 eggs	10 roubles	60 roubles
kg. of butter	3.5 roubles	200 roubles
pair of eyeglasses	8 roubles	200 roubles
pair of shoes	35 roubles	1,500 roubles
dental crown	100 roubles	8,000 roubles
color television	700 roubles	18,000 roubles

(Source: Department of Sociology, Armenian Academy of Sciences, Yerevan, Republic of Armenia, personal communication)

In 1993 Armenia introduced its own currency, the dram. This has failed to stabilize the economy, which continues to be devastated by the Azerbaijani blockade. The current period is also characterized by an extensive black market offering a wide variety of goods at prices that exclude most members of the citizenry.

4. International Monetary Fund, *Economic Review: Azerbaijan* (Washington, DC, 1992), pp. 14–15. In September 1994, Azerbaijan signed a $7 billion contract with a British Petroleum-led consortium for the sale of Azeri oil. However, the war over Karabagh has undoubtedly seriously harmed Azerbaijan. A portion of the country remains in the hands of Karabagh Armenian forces and one million Azeri refugees live in hastily constructed and poorly supplied camps.

5. The most violent post-Soviet conflict to date is the civil war in Tajikistan, which has claimed over 40,000 lives according to some reports.

6. Armenia's energy dependence is outlined in John Tedstrom, "Armenia: A Energy Profile," *Report on the U.S.S.R.* (22 February 1991), pp. 18–20.

7. International Monetary Fund, *Economic Review: Armenia* (Washington, DC, 1992), pp. 48–49.

8. Carolann S. Najarian, "When Artsakh Is Free, It Will Be a Great Victory over Injustice," *Armenian Mirror Spectator* (24 April 1993), p. 7. See also Celestine Bohlin, "Blockade and Winter Deepen Misery in Armenia," *New York Times* (7 February 1993), pp. 4, 12.

9. In 1994, the name was changed to the Organization for Security and Cooperation in Europe (OSCE).

10. Report of an International Delegation from the First International Andrei Sakharov Memorial Congress to Armenia and Azerbaijan (25–31 May 1991), unpublished manuscript.

11. Mark Saroyan, "The Karabagh Syndrome and Azerbaijani Politics," *Problems of Communism* (September/October 1990), pp. 18–20.

12. The Azerbaijani Communist Party defeated the Popular Front in elections as late as the fall of 1991.

13. Daniel Sneider, "Karabagh Residents Hunker Down for War," *Christian Science Monitor* (16 March 1992), p. 6.

14. "Unspeakable Fate for Armenians if Artsakh Falls," *Armenian Mirror Spectator* (29 February 1992), p. 11. Also see "Armenia Wins Major Victory over Azerbaijan," *The Current Digest*, vol. XLIV, no. 19 (1992), p. 7; and Tony Halpin, "Passage to Artsakh," *AIM* (June 1992), p. 14.

15. "Massacre by Armenians Being Reported," *New York Times* (3 March 1992), p. A–3.

16. "French Eyewitness Refutes Azeri Allegation of a Massacre in Khodjalu," *Armenian Mirror Spectator* (7 March 1992), p. 1; and "Former President Mutalibov Says Events in Khodjalu Were Manipulated by Azerbaijan Opposition," ibid., (25 April 1992), p. 16.

17. It should be pointed out that the borders of the present-day Mountainous Karabagh (the formal Soviet Azerbaijani region of the Nagorno-Karabagh Autonomous Oblast) are smaller than the territory of Mountainous Karabagh ceded to Azerbaijan by the Soviets in the early 1920s. The Lachin Strip and the Shahumian district were part of Mountainous Karabagh but were stripped away by the Azerbaijani authorities and administered directly as part of Azerbaijan.

18. During the Brezhnev years, Elchibey had served two years in hard labor, 1975–1976, for pro-Turkish activities.

19. Ronald Grigor Suny, "Bosnia in the Caucasus," *New York Times* (1 September 1992), op-ed page.

20. Paul A. Goble, a former U.S. State Department official and specialist on Soviet minorities now with the Carnegie Endowment for International Peace, has proposed that Armenia cede its southern land bridge separating Nakhichevan (the western, non-contiguous province of Azerbaijan sharing a border with Turkey) from Azerbaijan proper in return for access to Karabagh by way of the Lachin Strip. The State Department insists that Goble speaks as a private citizen. Paul A. Goble, "Coping with the Nagorno-Karabagh Crisis," *The Fletcher Forum of World Affairs*, vol. 16, no. 2 (Summer 1992), p. 26.

21. "Turkey Warned on Enclave," *Boston Globe* (21 May 1992), p. 2.

22. "Fascist Gray Wolves Spearhead Attack against Armenians in Artsakh," *Armenian Mirror Spectator* (25 July 1992), p. 1. Also see "Ankara Promises to Assist Turkish Republics and Train Their Armies," *Armenian Mirror Spectator* (11 January 1992), pp. 1, 16; and "Turkish Mercenaries in Artsakh," *Armenian Mirror Spectator* (11 April 1992), pp. 12–13. It was reported in late 1992 that the Gray Wolves had withdrawn back to Turkey. Patrick Gorman, "The Emerging Army in Azerbaijan," *Central Asia Monitor* (January/February 1993), p. 35

23. For a discussion of the limits of international peacekeeping efforts by the United Nations see Stephen Ryan, "Ethnic Conflict and the United Nations," *Ethnic and Racial Studies*, vol. 13 (January 1990), pp. 25–49.

24. Part of the reason for the success of the Karabagh Armenians is found in the motivation of the fighters. As Michael Specter tells us of Armenia, Azerbaijan, and Karabagh:

> For anybody who has spent time in both countries—and on the bleak, beautiful terrain for which they are fighting so viciously—it is impossible not to notice the difference in national resolve.

> . . . a woman, Lana Hayvaysian, 23, stood alone in the Stepanakert cemetery, smoothing black earth on the new grave of her husband. "He died so that this country can survive," she said, surrounded by hundreds of similar plots. "And we will survive. We will always survive."

> There is no such air of urgency in Azerbaijan, the far bigger, more powerful, and better supplied enemy. In Baku, the capital, people say openly that they are tired of the war for the province that they officially possess. . . . The Azerbaijanis want peace and wealth and the fruits of the West that their nearly immeasurable oil reserves will one day bring.

> In Stepanakert, the capital of Nagorno–Karabagh, it is literally impossible to find an able-bodied man—whether volunteer from Armenia or local resident—out of uniform. In Azerbaijan, draft-age men hang out in cafés all day long.

"Armenians Suffer Painfully in War, but with Pride and Determination," *The New York Times* (15 July 1994), p. A–3.

Appendix A

PROGRAM OF THE
KARABAGH COMMITTEE

Through the evolution of historical facts, Armenia be-came a member of a federation of peoples founded as a volun-tary union of sovereign republics and based on the principle of the self-determination of nations. In their internal as well as their foreign policies, the central authorities of the Union must promote the expression and defend the rights of all the repub-lics and nationalities in this multinational state.

Since February of 1988, the Karabagh Movement, which dates back to an earlier period, has enjoyed the support of the entire Armenian people. The movement was established to seek recognition for the natural and legitimate right of self-determi-nation for the Armenian people of Artsakh [Karabagh, trans.], a right that has been denied since 1921.

The objective of the Karabagh Movement is the reunification of Artsakh with Armenia. It is also concerned with all of the other major issues tied to the destiny of the Armenian people, including problems that appear at first not to be directly linked to the question of Karabagh.

The necessary precondition for the resolution of a vital na-tional issue, whatever it may be, is the awakening of a people and the organization of all of its resources and capabilities.

Of all the issues facing the Armenians, none has played a greater role in awakening and bringing together the Armenian people than the question of the reunification of Karabagh. A people who are reborn in struggle come to feel the pain of their other unresolved problems more acutely, and they come to understand that each problem is one link in a common chain. The solution to each problem moves us closer to the resolution of the others.

Each of the problems that the Karabagh Movement has brought to light is intimately related to the survival of our people. Some problems predated the February days, and as the movement grew and intensified, these issues were absorbed by the Karabagh Movement. As the movement developed, it moved beyond the limits imposed by the solution to any single problem, but at the same time it held true to its basic mission without deviation. The unification of Artsakh with Armenia served as the basis for a true national movement. This is demonstrated as much by the number of participants as by the number of problems the movement has brought to light.

The growth of the movement, its adaptation to new issues, and the active support of ever larger numbers of individuals convinced us of the necessity for a clearer organizational structure. With this objective in mind, the Karabagh Committee undertook to organize an Armenian National Movement while maintaining the original designation of the Karabagh Movement up until the reunification of Artsakh with Armenia.

Before dealing with the question of organizational structure, we wish to outline the principles of our movement. These principles flow naturally from the historical experience of the Armenian people, and they have become even more deeply aware of them given the events of the past six months.

Let us examine the objectives of the Armenian National Movement and the modes of action we believe will enable us to achieve them.

IDEOLOGICAL PRINCIPLES OF THE ARMENIAN NATIONAL MOVEMENT

1. It is undeniable that the Armenians, like all nationalities, have known how to mobilize their resources to the fullest

and to contribute to the progress of civilization when they have lived freely and democratically and been able to make their own decisions concerning their economic, social, and cultural systems without outside interference.

It is clear that only under these conditions can individuals exercise their natural rights including the principal ones of the right to life, personal liberty, and the pursuit of happiness.

2. The will of the people is sovereign and is expressed through the ballot box and by means of laws voted upon by a freely elected parliament.

Repression of the popular will is a violation of the right to self-determination as defined by international standards.

3. The principal guarantor of the future of our nation is the Armenian language which is not only a means of communication but also the expression of a mode of thinking and of a culture and a political life.

4. To achieve its national objectives, the Armenian people rely on their own resources and do not count on the guardianship of others, for as history has proven, that only throws us into dependency and moral bondage. To think that a nation can have an eternal friend or an eternal enemy constitutes backward thinking and underdeveloped thought.

5. We reject these immoral and sterile political viewpoints as the basis for our nation's diplomacy, because on the one hand it requires an entire people to pledge fidelity and submission to another, while on the other hand it encourages hostility toward other peoples and religions.

6. Our movement is not directed against any people. Our goal is to live in peace and harmony with all our neighbors. But we are convinced that peace and harmony cannot be consolidated and strengthened unless it is founded upon justice and unless it does not infringe upon the rights of any other people.

7. At the moment, national and state interests play a much more important role in the relations between peoples than similarities or differences in religion.

The time for holy wars is past. Equally, ideologies that seek to unify all peoples of the same stock—such as pan-Turkism, Arab unity, pan-Slavism, etc.—have lost their political force. Today international relations are not based on ethnic or religious groups but on the recognition of common economic, ideological, or military interests.

8. Exterior forces certainly play an important role in the history of a people, but it is dangerous for a people to only seek the causes of its successes and setbacks in such factors. This can lead to the breakup of a people and to its self-destruction. Unfavorable conditions and outside pressure can force a people into retreat, but nations that maintain their faith in the future and their moral and spiritual strength and employ them at critical moments are not only assured of their national existence but also of the fulfillment of their objectives.

9. We are in solidarity with all movements that are founded on the principles of self-determination, democracy, and social justice. We reject all manifestations of discrimination and national fanaticism

THE SHORT-TERM OBJECTIVES OF THE ARMENIAN NATIONAL MOVEMENT

The primary objective of our movement has been and remains the unification of Artsakh with Armenia. The fulfillment of this objective is intimately linked to the resolution of other questions vital to the Armenian people. That is why the Armenian National Movement feels it is urgent that the following objectives be achieved in the near future. Each of these, taken by itself, is significant in assuring the survival of the Armenian people and for the accomplishment of its major objectives.

1. To extend the sovereignty of our Republic by carrying out the essential measures defined below:

* To guarantee, by means of sound management and self-financing, the economic autonomy of the Republic.

* To restore the unity of Armenian national forces.

* To rely on Article 80 of the Constitution of the U.S.S.R. to establish diplomatic relations and an exchange of embassies between the Republic of Armenia and those nations which have large Armenian diasporan communities.

2. To work toward the affirmation and deepening of democracy in our country, in the interests of the people, in the full

knowledge that only democratic conditions can serve as the basis for the true resolution of problems that confront the Armenian National Movement.

3. To rigorously apply Article 72 of the Constitution with regard to the official language of the Republic. With this objective in mind, to pass laws that favor the defense of the Armenian language.

4. To seek to ensure that all children in the Armenian Republic in all schools receive their education in Armenian and to adopt measures favoring the use of Armenian by Armenians living outside the Republic.

5. To lead an uncompromising struggle for the protection of nature and against pollution with the full understanding that the seriousness of the ecological situation is not only a threat to the health and well being of our youth but also a risk to the physical and mental health of generations to come. The first priority here is the closure of central nuclear facilities and the closing of the chemical production complex at Nairit.

6. To seek the recognition of the Armenian genocide by the Supreme Soviets of Armenia and the Soviet Union and by the United Nations.

7. To proclaim April 24th in Armenia the national day of remembrance of the Armenian genocide. This day will be an annual day of commemoration and a public holiday.

8. To bring to the fore historical Armenian claims to certain territories and to insist that these territories be reattached to Armenia. The validity of Armenian claims to these territories is proven by international documents. It is understood, however, that these claims can only be realized through a national political struggle based on the principles of our movement.

9. To reevaluate Armenian political movements from earlier historical periods and to reassess their major figures.

10. To declare May 28th a national holiday in commemoration of the restoration of Armenian independence [1918, trans.] and to adopt the tricolor flag of the independent Armenian Republic as a national symbol.

11. The Armenian National Movement includes all Armenians.

12. To guarantee the free operation of Armenian churches,

to open new churches upon request of the faithful, and to reestablish national religious holidays and traditions.

13. To insist on the renaming of cities and villages of the Republic of Armenia by their traditional historical names.

These articles may be amended according to suggestions and criticisms by the members of our movement.

MEANS OF ACTION FOR THE
ARMENIAN NATIONAL MOVEMENT

From the beginning the Armenian people have expressed their desire for the reunification of Artsakh with Armenia. The Armenian National Movement, growing out of the Karabagh Movement, has therefore adopted the following principles:

1. To promote all rights accorded by the Constitution; that is, to actively participate in all elections from the local to the national level so that the true will of the people will be expressed through these elections and to dismiss deputies who misrepresent or fail to express this will. In case of need, the population will be heard by means of meetings, demonstrations, or strikes.

2. To revise current Constitutional articles that hinder democratic participation and introduce new articles that conform to democratic principles.

3. To struggle against laws and decrees that are in contradiction with the spirit of the Constitution and the interests of the people by revising these articles.

4. If the situation arises and if there is not a contradiction in modes of action, political principles, and objectives, the Armenian National Movement can work with other national organizations to seek a solution to our national problems.

5. In the course of democratic and national struggle, the movement is ready to work with the authorities of the Republic at all times that their actions are consistent with the national interests of the Armenian people.

6. Besides demonstrations and meetings, the Armenian National Movement must have other means of communicating

with the popular masses—especially in writing—such as news sources, periodicals, files, and documents.

ORGANIZATIONAL STRUCTURE OF THE ARMENIAN NATIONAL MOVEMENT

We believe it would be a mistake to think of the movement as part of an unchanging world. Its structure must resemble that of a living organism which develops and modifies itself as the problems it is presented with are resolved. Thus each participant has the possibility of using the ingenuity and spirit of initiative that characterize our people.

Beyond the acceptance of these principles, modes of action, and objectives of the movement, each person is free to decide upon his or her level and type of action.

Let us look at the lines of organizational command for the movement.

1. A general assembly examines the principles of the Armenian National Movement, its objectives and its modes of action.

Those who accept these can form groups and each of these can be designated as a member group of the Movement. They will elect a council, which will inform the proper representative of the Movement of these elections.

In case of circumstances or other necessity, members of the groups may, after having informed the national committee, set themselves up as local associations or specialists in a particular sector.

2. Existing public organizations or new organizations that desire to participate in the movement may be recognized upon accepting the statutes of the Armenian National Movement and coming to a mutual agreement with the Movement representative.

3. Each may become a full member of the movement by adhering to the organization outlined above.

4. In all cities and regions of Armenia as well as in all places where Armenians are found outside of the Republic, organizational and support groups of the Movement may develop in the same manner and with the advice of the movement.

The first Armenian National Council will be created by the representatives of the regional committees and organizations with the participation and assistance of the committee. This Council will develop the programs and organizational structure of the movement in greater detail as well as provide leadership for it.

Until the creation of the National Council, the organization will be directed by the Committee of the Karabagh Movement.

The Armenian Committee of the Karabagh Movement

Yerevan, 19 August 1989

Appendix B

CHRONOLOGY 1878 – 7 JANUARY 1989

1878   Treaties of San Stefano and Berlin. Intervention by the European powers on behalf of the Armenians in the Ottoman Empire.

1887–   Founding of the Hnchak and Dashnak Armenian po-
1890   litical movements.

1895–   Massacres of Armenians in the Ottoman Empire un-
1896   der Sultan Abdul Hamid.

1908   Institutional revolution carried out by the Committee of Union and Progress led by the Young Turks.

1909   Renewed massacres of Armenians in Cilicia.

1914   Beginning of World War I. The Ottoman Empire joins the Central Powers: Germany and Austria–Hungary.

1915–   Mass deportation and liquidation of Anatolian Arme-
1916   nians, 40 to 50 percent of whom (between 600,000 and 1.1 million) are killed out of a population of 1.5 to 2 million.

1918   End of World War I. Collapse of the Ottoman Empire. Founding of the Republic of Armenia in the Transcaucasus.

1919   Unionist trials. Talaat, Enver, and Djemal, the triumvirate heads of the Ottoman Empire, are sentenced to death *in absentia* by an Ottoman court.

1920   Treaty of Sèvres. Sovietization of Armenia.

1921   Assassination of the Young Turk leader Talaat in Berlin. His assassin Tehlerian is acquitted. Soviet leaders deny Armenian claims and assign the territories of Mountainous Karabagh and Nakhichevan to Azerbaijan.

1923   Mustapha Kemal founds the Republic of Turkey. Treaty of Lausanne.

1945   Nuremberg Tribunal.

1948   International Convention on Genocide (United Nations).

1965   Non-official demonstration in Yerevan (capital of Soviet Armenia) on the occasion of the 50th anniversary of the genocide.

1973–   A preliminary report of the United Nations Sub-
1974   Commission on Human Rights concerning the prevention and repression of the crime of genocide mentions the Armenian massacres in 1915 as the first genocide of the twentieth century and becomes the object of a procedural battle. The Turkish delegate demands a revision of the paragraph mentioning the Armenian case.

1975   Commemoration of the 60th anniversary of the genocide. Demonstrations throughout the world. The beginning of attacks on Turkish diplomats.

1978–
1979
The document concerning the preservation and repression of the crime of genocide is presented to the
United Nations Sub-Commission on Human Rights
(of which Turkey is a member). Paragraph 30 mentioning the Armenian case is censored. The report is
presented again in 1979 without Paragraph 30. A
procedural struggle begins.

1975–
1982
A series of assassinations throughout the world claims
the lives of about thirty members of the Turkish diplomatic corps (and sometimes members of their families). Two clandestine Armenian organizations are
responsible: the Justice Commandos of the Armenian
Genocide and the Armenian Secret Army for the Liberation of Armenia (ASALA). The first is associated
with the Dashnak Party and the second is third
worldist.

1983
ASALA (Orly faction) carries out a particularly odi-
ous action against the Turkish national airline causing
the death of eight passengers. The Armenian diaspora
and its organizations register their unanimous disapproval. Assassination attempts cease worldwide.

1984
The Permanent People's Tribunal convenes in Paris
to consider the Armenian genocide. The jury includes
three Nobel Prize winners: Sean MacBride of Ireland,
Adolfo Perez Esquivel of Argentina, and George
Wald of the United States.

1986
The United Nations Sub-Commission on Human
Rights accepts Ben Whitaker's report on the prevention and repression of the crime of genocide. The
report mentions the massacre of Armenians.

1987
A moral victory for the Armenians. The Council of
Europe recognizes the genocide and suggests that
Turkey do likewise. Beginning of the summer: Armenians are worried about an alarmist article on the
subject of dangerous pollution emissions by chemical
factories in Yerevan.

1 September: First demonstrations for ecology in Armenia. Several weeks later, the Armenians also demand the re-unification of Mountainous Karabagh with the Republic of Armenia.

1988   *19–26 February:* Demonstrations in Yerevan bringing together, on some days, close to a million people on ecological and territorial issues. The Karabagh Committee forms at this time.

26 February: Mr. Gorbachev, Secretary General of the Communist Party, asks for a one month moratorium in which to formulate a policy. The Armenians suspend their demonstrations.

27–29 February: The Azerbaijanis murder several dozen Armenians in Sumgait. The authorities do not intervene for three days.

25 March: At the end of the moratorium period, Mr. Gorbachev answers *nyet* without concession to the Armenians.

26 March: The Armenians register their disapproval by means of a one day "dead city" protest in Yerevan. Gorbachev's denial radicalizes Armenian national aspirations.

28–29 June: The Armenians are disappointed by the XIXth Congress of the Communist Party. The government again refuses all concessions. This blunt refusal unleashes a new general strike.

5 July: The army kills an Armenian while dispersing a peaceful demonstration at the Zvartnots International Airport in Yerevan. This contributes to the development of anti-Russian sentiments in Armenia.

12 July: The deputies in Mountainous Karabagh unilaterally decide in favor of the reunification of their region with the Republic of Armenia.

18 July: The televised session of the Supreme Soviet devoted to nationalities shatters all illusions and leads to the growth of "anti-Gorbachevism" in Armenia. The Karabagh Committee publishes a program that goes beyond territorial reunification to advocate the institution of liberal democracy.

9 September: 150,000 to 200,000 Armenians demand independence while hoisting their national flag.

7 November: On the occasion of the commemoration of the 1917 Revolution, nearly a million Armenians jeer Party leaders while favoring the Karabagh Committee. From this day on we see a system of dual power or "alternative" power in Soviet Armenia.

24 November: The authorities increase the pressure in Armenia by declaring a state of emergency.

7 December: In the Leninakan, Spitak, Kirovakan, and Stepanavan region, at 11:41 a.m., local time, the first earthquake tremor, with a magnitude of 6.9, and a second tremor at 11:45, with a magnitude of 5.8.

As consequence of the earthquake, there are at least 100,000 dead, constituting 3.03 percent of the Armenians living in Soviet Armenia.

Soviet and foreign relief workers are not able to free more than 80 survivors from the rubble. The disaster leaves between 500,000 and 700,000 disaster victims. From right after the earthquake until 9:15 p.m. on 9 December, relief is provided by the survivors in their immediate environment. On the afternoon of the 7th, practically the entire Karabagh Committee goes to the disaster area and estimates the human losses and needs of the survivors. That night, on returning to Yerevan, the Committee informs Agence France-

Presse of its estimate of human losses (100,000 dead), coordinates aid, including foreign aid, and carries on without interruption until 10 December at 6:20 p.m. The Soviet army, omnipresent, does not directly participate in the relief effort. In France, late in the morning on 7 December, the operational center of Public Safety learns of the catastrophe. They verify the information in the afternoon and take inventory of their available rescue equipment and supplies. In the evening, two disaster intervention planes (DICA) are placed on alert.

8 December: In the early hours of the morning, two DICA planes belonging to Public Safety are ready to take off for Armenia. They await authorization from the Soviets.

9 a.m.: Five physicians are ready to leave for the disaster areas. They wait for their visas until noon on December 10th and at the end of the day board the first Doctors without Borders plane departing for Armenia.

SOS/Armenia is established.

Doctors without Borders gives its visa requests to the Soviet authorities in Paris and gathers its relief materials.

7 p.m.: The Soviet authorities approve French governmental assistance.

December 9th, 5:40 a.m. (French time): The first units of the French relief detachment take off from France for Armenia. They land the same day at 4 p.m. (local time) in Yerevan and arrive in Leninakan at 9:15 p.m. French governmental aid consists of 499 people, 55 dogs, 77.5 tons of material. The French rescue workers will save 15 people. Doctors without Borders mobilizes its United European Intervention Program and obtains, that night, authorization to deliver relief.

10 December: Mr. Gorbachev arrives in Yerevan and spends the day there in meetings.

6:20 p.m.: While they are coordinating aid for the victims, 7 of the 11 official members of the Karabagh Committee are arrested: A. Manoutcharian, S. Guevorguian, B. Ararktsian, S. Ghazarian, A. Hakobian, V. Manoukian, L. Ter Petrossian. They are sentenced to thirty days in prison with the exception of A. Manoutcharian, released because he is a parliamentary deputy.

9 p.m.: The first Doctors without Borders plane takes off from Brussels for Armenia carrying 11 members of DWB and 30 tons of cargo.

11 December 11, 7 a.m.: The first Doctors without Borders plane lands in Yerevan. Part of the supplies are left there for use in local hospitals and the rest is taken to Leninakan.

12 December: Doctors without Borders opens its first dispensary in Leninakan. They treat 350 to 400 patients a day until the end of the month.

13 December: In Leninakan, cars equipped with loudspeakers order the population to evacuate the disaster areas. V. Siradeghian, a member of the Karabagh Committee, is jailed.

14 December: The Soviet government orders the detachment of French relief workers to leave Spitak.

15 December: 152 relief workers in the French detachment leave Armenia.

16 December: There is growing anguish and suffering among the victims.

17 December: Doctors without Borders opens its second dispensary in Leninakan. The last group of French relief workers leaves Armenia.

18 December: The survivors begin their mourning period for the deceased.

20 December: The work of clearing the rubble begins.

21–30 December: As burials proceed, coffins begin to disappear from Leninakan.

22 December: Dynamiting of damaged buildings begins in Leninakan. Because the people are slow in obeying orders to evacuate buildings, the government cuts the distribution of food, natural gas, and other essentials.

25 December: Doctors without Borders begins to observe cases of psychiatric deterioration among the survivors. Around this same time, Armenians see visions of the Virgin Mary several kilometers from Leninakan.

1989 *1 January:* Doctors without Borders opens its third dispensary in Leninakan.

7 January: The last four official members of the Karabagh Committee are jailed: A. Manoutcharian, R. Ghazarian, H. Galoustian, D. Vardanian. By this time, nearly 300 Committee activists are behind bars. And by this date, the authorities have not assumed responsibility for assistance to the victims and have left their care to foreign humanitarian aid.

This chronology was compiled by Gérard Chaliand (from 1878 to 1987) and Pierre Verluise (from the summer of 1987 to 7 January 1989).

Selected Bibliography

General History

Jacques De Morgan, *Histoire du peuple arménien* (Marseilles: Université de Marseille, 1980).

Gérard Dedeyan (under the direction of), *Histoire des Arméniens* (Toulouse: Privat, 1986).

Sirapie Der Nersessian, *The Armenians* (New York: Praeger, 1970).

Patrick Donabedian and J. M. Thierry, *Les Arts arméniens* (Paris: Mazenod, 1987).

René Grousset, *Histoire de l'Arménie des origines à 1071* (Paris: Payot, 1988).

David Marshall Lang, *Armenia: Cradle of Civilization* (London: George Allen & Unwin, 1970).

_____, *The Armenians: A People in Exile* (London: Unwin Paperbacks, 1988).

Claude Mutafian, *La Cilicie au carrefour des empires*, 2 vols. (Paris: Les Belles Lettres, 1988).

H. Pasdermadjian, *Histoire de l'Arménie depuis les orgines jusqu'au traité de Lausanne* (Paris: Librairie Samuelian, 1971).

Ronald Grigor Suny, *Armenia in the 20th Century* (Chico, CA: Scholars Press, 1983).

Ronald Grigor Suny, ed., *Transcaucasia, Nationalism and Social Change: Essays in the History of Armenia, Azerbaijan, and Georgia* (Ann Arbor: Michigan Slavic Publications, 1983).

Anahide Ter Minassian, *La Question arménienne* (Marseilles: Parenthèses, 1983).

Armenians in the Ottoman Empire under Sultan Abdul Hamid and the Massacres of 1895–1896

Le Livre jaune, Affaires arméniennes (1893–1897) and *Supplément* (1895–1896) (Paris: Ministry of Foreign Affairs, 1897).

Archival and Eyewitness Accounts Concerning the Mass Deportation and Liquidation of Anatolian Armenians (1915–1916)

Aram Andonian, *The Memoirs of Naim Bey: Turkish Official Documents Relating to the Deportations and Massacres of Armenians* (London: Hodder & Stoughton, 1920).

The Armenian Genocide: Documentation, 2 vols. (Munich: Institut für Armenische Fragen, 1988).

A. Beylerian, *L'Empire ottoman, les Grandes Puissances et les Arméniens dans les archives françaises* (Paris: Publications de la Sorbonne, 1982).

J. Bryce, and Arnold Toynbee, *Livre bleu sur les massacres des Arméniens dans l'Empire ottoman* (Paris: Payot, 1987). (*The Treatment of Armenians in the Ottoman Empire*, London: J. Causton and Sons, 1916.)

Vahakn Dadrian, *Documentation of the Armenian Genocide in German and Austrian Sources* (New Brunswick, NJ: Transaction Books, 1994).

Leslie Davis, *The Slaughterhouse Province: An American Diplomat's Report on the Armenian Genocide, 1915–1917* (New Rochelle, NY: Aristide D. Caratzas, 1989).

Richard Hovannisian, *The Armenian Holocaust: A Bibliography Relating to the Deportations, Massacres, and Dispersion of the Armenian People, 1915–1923* (Cambridge, MA: Armenian Heritage Press, National Association for Armenian Studies and Research, 1981).

Johannes Lepsius, *Archives du génocide des Arméniens* (Paris: Fayard, 1986), preface by Alfred Grosser (original in German, 1918).

_____, *Deutschland und Armenien, 1914–1918* (Potsdam: Der Tempelverlag, 1919).

_____, *Rapport secret sur les massacres d'Arménie* (Paris: Payot, 1987), preface by Paul Thibaud (original in German, 1916).

Donald E. Miller and Lorna T. Miller, *Survivors: An Oral History of the Armenian Genocide*, Berkeley and Los Angeles: University of California Press, 1993.

Hans Morgenthau, *Mémoires, suivi de Documents du département d'Etat* (Paris: Flammarion, 1983), preface by Gérard Chaliand. (*Ambassador Morgenthau's Story*, Garden City, NY: Doubleday, Page & Co., 1926.)

Arnold Toynbee, *Les Massacres d'Arménie* (Paris: Payot, 1987). (*Armenian Atrocities: The Murder of a Nation*, London: Hodder and Stoughton, 1915.)

German Witnesses

Martin Niepage, *The Horrors of Aleppo Seen by a German Eyewitness* (New York: George H. Doran Co., 1918).

Stürmer, *Deux ans à Constantinople* (Paris: Payot, 1917) (original in German 1917).

Armin T. Wegner, *Offner Brief an den Präsidenten des Vereinigen Staaten von Nord-America, Herrn Woodrow Wilson über die Austreibung des Armenischen Volkes in die Wüste* (Berlin: O. Fleck, 1919).

Concerning the Genocide

J. M. Carzou, *Un génocide exemplaire, Arménie, 1915* (Paris: Flammarion, 1975; Brussels: Marabout, 1980).

Gérard Chaliand, and Yves Ternon, *Le Génocide des Arméniens* (Brussels: Complexe, 1980). (*The Armenians: From Genocide to Resistance*, London: Zed Books, 1983.)

Gérard Chaliand, ed., *Tribunal permanent des peuples. Le crime de silence* (Paris, "Champs" Flammarion, 1984), preface by P. Vidal–Naquet. (Gerard Libaridian, ed., *Permanent People's Tribunal, A Crime of Silence: The Armenian Genocide*, London: Zed Books,, 1985.)

Vahakn N. Dadrian, "Genocide as a Problem of National and International Law: The World War I Armenian Case and Its Contemporary Legal Ramifications," *Yale Journal of International Law*, 14: 2 (Summer 1989), pp. 221–334.

_____, "The Naim-Andonian Documents on the World War I Destruction of Ottoman Armenians: The Anatomy of a Genocide," *International Journal of Middle East Studies*, 18 (1986), pp. 311–360.

_____, "The Structural–Functional Components of Genocide: A Victimological Approach to the Armenian Case," in *Victimology*, vol. II, ed. by I. Drapkin and E. Viano (Lexington, MA: Lexington Books, D.C. Heath and Company, 1974).

Jacques Der Alexanian, *Le ciel était noir sur l'Euphrate* (Paris: Robert Laffont, 1988).

Esprit, special issue, *Arménie, Le Droit à la mémoire* (April 1984).

Ephraim Jernazian, *Judgment Unto Truth: Witnessing the Armenian Genocide* (New Brunswick, NJ: Transaction Publishers, 1990).

David Marshall Lang and Christopher J. Walker, *Les Arméniens*, preface by Yves Ternon, afterword by Claude Gambiez (Paris: Minority Rights Group, 1979 and 1980). (This differs considerably from the original English version, *The Armenians*, London: Minority Rights Group, 1977 and 1978.)

Paul Saba, "The Armenian National Question" in Berch Berberoglu, ed., *Power and Stability in the Middle East* (London: Zed Books,, 1989), pp. 173–201.

Ervin Staub, *The Roots of Evil: The Origins of Genocide and Other Group Violence* (Cambridge: Cambridge University Press, 1989).

Les Temps Modernes, special issue, *Arménie/Diaspora, Mémoire et Modernité* (July–September 1988).

Yves Ternon, *Les Arméniens, histoire d'un génocide* (Paris: Seuil, 1977). (*The Armenians: History of a Genocide*, Delmar, NY: Caravan Books, 1990.)

_____, *La Cause arménienne* (Paris: Seuil, 1981). (*The Armenian Cause*, Delmar, NY: Caravan Books, 1985.)

_____, *Enquête sur la négation d'un génocide* (Marseilles: Parenthèses, 1989).

Ulrich Trumpener, *Germany and the Ottoman Empire, 1914–1918* (Princeton: Princeton University Press, 1968).

Christopher Walker, *Armenia: Survival of a Nation*, revised edition (New York: St. Martins, 1990).

Franz Werfel, *Les 40 jours du Musa-Dagh* (Paris: Albin Michel, 1986), preface by Elie Wiesel (reedition). (*The 40 Days of Musa Dagh*, New York: Viking, 1934).

Turkish Allegations at the Time of the Events

Aspirations et Agissements révolutionnaires des Comités arméniens (Constantinople: 1917).

Bey Ahmed Rustem, *La Guerre mondiale et la Question turco-arménienne* (Bern: 1918).

Schemsi Kara, *Turcs et Arméniens devant l'Histoire* (Geneva: 1919).

Recent Turkish Publications

Cemal Öskaya Inayetullah, *Le Peuple arménien et les Tentatives de réduire le peuple turc en servitude* (Istanbul: Institute for Turkish Studies, 1971).

Kamuran Gurun, *Le Dossier arménien* (Istanbul: 1984). (*The Armenian File*, New York: St. Martins, 1986).

Historians Defending the Turkish Position

Justin McCarthy, *Muslims and Minorities: The Population of Ottoman Anatolia and the End of the Empire* (New York: New York University Press, 1983).

Responses to Turcophile Writers including Justin McCarthy

David Davidian, *Addressing Turkish Genocide Apologists*, 4 vols. (Cambridge, MA: The Social Democratic Party of Armenia, 1989).

Levon Marashlian, *Politics and Demography: Armenians, Turks, and Kurds in the Ottoman Empire* (New Rochelle, NY: Aristide D. Caratzas, 1990).

E. K. Sarkisian and R. G. Sahakian, *Vital Issues in Modern Armenian History* (Watertown, MA: Armenian Studies, 1965).

The Situation of Armenians on the Eve of the First World War

Serge Afanasyan, *L'Arménie, la Géorgie, l'Azerbaïdjan de l'indépendence à la soviétisation* (Paris: l'Harmattan, 1981).

_____, *La Victoire de Sardarabad* (Paris: l'Harmattan, 1985).

A. Chiragian, *La Dette de sang. Un Arménien traque les responsables du génocide* (Paris: Ramsay, 1982, Brussels: Complexe, 1985), preface by Gérard Chaliand.

Jacques Derogy, *Opération Némésis. Les Vengeurs arméniens* (Paris: Fayard, 1986), preface by Gérard Chaliand. (*Resistance and Revenge*, New Brunswick, NJ: Transaction Books, 1990.)

Richard Hovannisian, *Armenia on the Road to Independence* (Berkeley and Los Angeles: University of California Press, 1967).

_____, *The Republic of Armenia*, 2 vols. (Los Angeles and London: University of California Press, 1971 and 1982).

Richard Hovannisian, ed., *The Armenian Genocide in Perspective* (New Brunswick, NJ: Transaction Books, 1986).

Stanley E. Kerr, *The Lions of Marash. Personal Experiences with American Near-East Relief, 1919–1922* (Albany: State University of New York Press, 1973).

Raymond Kevorkian and Paul B. Paboudjian, *Les Arméniens dans l'Empire ottoman à la veille du génocide* (Paris: Les Editions d'Art et d'Histoire, 1993).

A. Krikorian, *Justicier du génocide arménien, le procès de Tehlirian* (Paris: éditions Kirk, 1982) (original in German). (*The Case of Soghomon Tehlirian*, Los Angeles: Asbarez Publishing Company, 1985.)

Mandelstam, *La Société des Nations et les Puissances devant le problème arménien* (Paris: 1926).

Fridjof Nansen, *Rapport sur la situation de l'Arménie* (Geneva: 1925). (*Armenia and the Near East*, New York: Duffield and Co., 1928.)

Rapport du Near-East Relief, bilingual English–French edition (Marseilles: Parenthèses, 1984).

Anahide Ter Minassian, *La République d'Arménie (1918–1920)* (Brussels: Complexe, 1989).

Mountainous Karabakh and the Earthquake

George Bournoutian, *A History of Qarabagh: An Annotated Translation of Mirza Jamal Javanshir Qarabaghi's Tarikh-e Qarabagh* (Costa Mesa, CA: Mazda Publishers, 1994).

Levon Chorbajian, Patrick Donabedian, and Claude Mutufian, *The Caucasian Knot: The History and Geopolitics of Nagorno–Karabagh* (London: Zed Books, 1994).

Lady Baroness Caroline Cox and John Eibner, *Ethnic Cleansing in*

Progress: War in Nagorno-Karabakh (Washington, DC: Christian Solidarity International, 1993).

Editors of the Novosti Press Agency, *The Armenian Earthquake Disaster* (Madison, CT: Sphinx Books, 1989). (Originally in Russian.)

Glasnost, #1 (Paris: 1989).

Gerard Libaridian, *The Karabakh File, Documents and Facts on the Question of Mountainous Karabakh, 1918–1988* (Cambridge, MA: The Zoryan Institute, 1988).

Yuri Rost, *Armenian Tragedy* (New York: St. Martins, 1990), foreword by Andrei Sakharov.

Samvel Shahmuratian, *The Sumgait Tragedy: Pogroms against Armenians in Soviet Azerbaijan* (New Rochelle, NY: Aristide D. Caratzas, 1990), foreword by Yelena Bonner.

The Late Soviet and Post-Soviet Era

Gerard J. Libaridian, ed., *Armenia at the Crossroads: Democracy and Nationalism in the Post Soviet Era* (Cambridge, MA: Blue Crane, 1991).

Ronald Suny, "Incomplete Revolution: National Movements and the Collapse of the Soviet Empire," *New Left Review*, # 189 (September–October 1991), pp. 111–125.

_____, "The Revenge of the Past: Socialism and Ethnic Conflict in Transcaucasia," *New Left Review*, # 184 (October–November 1990), pp. 5–34.

Compiled by Gérard Chaliand and Levon Chorbajian

Index